The book of
Inspiration
for women by women

created by
Ruth Cyster-Stuettgen

First published by Busybird Publishing 2017
Copyright © 2017 Ruth Cyster-Stuettgen

ISBN 978-1-925585-59-9

Ruth Cyster-Stuettgen has asserted her right under the Copyright, Designs and Patents Act 1988 to be identified as the creator of this work. The information in this book is based on the authors' experiences and opinions. The publisher specifically disclaims responsibility for any adverse consequences, which may result from use of the information contained herein. Permission to use information has been sought by the author. Any breaches will be rectified in further editions of the book.

All rights reserved. No part of this publication may be reproduced, stored in or introduced into a retrieval system, or transmitted in any form, or by any means (electronic, mechanical, photocopying, recording or otherwise) without the prior written permission of the authors. Any person who does any unauthorized act in relation to this publication may be liable to criminal prosecution and civil claims for damages. Enquiries should be made through the publisher.

Cover image by Ali-P Art Northern Ireland
Cover design by Busybird Publishing
Layout and typesetting: Busybird Publishing

Busybird Publishing
2/118 Para Road
Montmorency VIC
Australia 3094
www.busybird.com.au

I am incredibly smitten, proud and honoured to be
surrounded by strong and inspirational women and girls.
Bringing *The Book of Inspiration for Women by Women* to life has only
been possible because of them. On behalf of all the contributors,
I humbly dedicate this book to all the women and girls who have
walked before us, are walking with us and will walk with us in
the future, on this journey called Life. May you be inspired to live
your life the fullest always, listening to the calling in your heart.

Contents

Introduction

Inspiration 001: Just Breathe, Nisha Ukani

Inspiration 002: You are Enough, Sarah Huon

Inspiration 003: Summer Solstice, Emma Sidney

Inspiration 004: You are Destined to Succeed, Christy Amalu

Inspiration 005: You are Wise, Diana Rickman

Inspiration 006: Self Worth, April Livingstone

Inspiration 007: Honour Family, Emily Stuettgen

Inspiration 008: Something Inside so Strong, Andrea Maynard-Brade

Inspiration 009: Differences, Natasha Hogan

Inspiration 010: Just Because I am a Daughter…, Ritu Sharma

Inspiration 011: Dream

Inspiration 012: Touched by Crisis, Luciane Sperling

Inspiration 013: What is Love, Anyway? Maddison Ellerton

Inspiration 014: The Power of Prayer, Dr Linet Amalie

Inspiration 015: Find Your "Why", Shari Ware

Inspiration 016: Sisterhood, Carol Ray

Inspiration 017: Distinction Takes Time, Suzanne Johnson

Inspiration 018: The Pursuit of Authenticity, Vicki McClifty

Inspiration 019: No Wound Too Great, Deb Ware

Inspiration 020: Feelings

Inspiration 021: You Too Can Survive, Maxine Harris-Burton

Inspiration 022: To My Sisters With Love, Emma Sidney

Inspiration 023: Be a Queen, Desh Dixon

Inspiration 024: Trust the Road Less Traveled, Stacie Coleman

Inspiration 025: Bubbles, Gameeda Henry

Inspiration 026: Intentions to Fly, Mel Williams

Inspiration 027: Life is Painful, Suffering is Optional, Marg Lange

Inspiration 028: Pay it Forward, Jerry Penny

Inspiration 029: Get Out of Your Head and Back Into Your Gut, Marylin Schirmer

Inspiration 030: Be Yourself, Blaise van Hecke

Inspiration 031: Be The Boss of Your Life, Tekka-Lee Williams

Inspiration 032: Inspiration

Inspiration 033: Self Love, Margaret Ioannidis

Inspiration 034: Contemplation, Roz Tilley

Inspiration 035: Going Deeper…, Jutta Maria Hecht

Inspiration 036: No Compromises, Laura Stuettgen

Inspiration 037: Be Your Best, Georgia Van Der Poel

Inspiration 038: Never Give Up, Emily Buckley-Fourter

Inspiration 039: Mind Matters, Vanita Dahia

Inspiration 040: A Goddess's encounter with Love, Luisa Russo

Inspiration 041: I'm Loving …

Inspiration 042: Crossroads, Tanya Chambers

Inspiration 043: Career Choices, Cille Harris

Inspiration 044: Just Get Started, Jessica Savic

Inspiration 045: Strive for Contentment, Tracey Maclay

Inspiration 046: You Can Only Control You, Robyn Nelson

Inspiration 047: The Butterfly Effect, Jo Schutt

Inspiration 048: Be Inspired, Blaise van Hecke

Inspiration 049: Baby Steps, Gaya Pedris

Inspiration 050: Miracles 3, Gaya Pedris

Inspiration 051: A Wise Woman, Andrea Rodriguez

Inspiration 052: Are You Being Selfish? Trish Springsteen

Inspiration 053: Something Good for Someone Else, Julie White

Inspiration 054: AHA! AHA! Moment in Collaboration, Carol-Chantal Séguin

Inspiration 055: Legacy Of An Abundant Life…, Yolanda Alvares

Inspiration 056: Truth, Adrienne Gaha-Morris

Inspiration 057: Cycles of Life, Roz Tilley

Inspiration 058: Becoming Change, Hannah Nicholson

Inspiration 059: You Are Perfect, Jose Toussaint

Inspiration 060: Self-Belief, Georgia Varjas

Inspiration 061: Dear Mum – Thank You, Lani Sharp

Inspiration 062: Sisters…, Ashleigh Andrews

Inspiration 063: Today and Tomorrow, Monika Miller

Inspiration 064: Your HEART Matters, Gill Barham

Inspiration 065: Never Give Up!, Marie Ferguson

Inspiration 066: Moving Forward, Ana-Rosa Avendano

Inspiration 067: Follow Your Passion, Marilou Coombe

Inspiration 068: Ignite Your Light, Nikki Simmos

Inspiration 069: Make Good Choices, Lynda Holt

Inspiration 070: Letting Go!, Maurissa Ailion

Inspiration 071: Growing in Kindness and Love, Joahnne Sperling

Inspiration 072: Girls, We Got This! Josie Kearsey

Inspiration 073: Proud to Be a Woman, Sonja Koukounaras

Inspiration 074: Connection to Self, Shani Suttie

Inspiration 075: Suddenly Homeless, Annie Toscher

Inspiration 076: Attitude is Everything, Elaine Squiers

Inspiration 077: In my Youth, I Wish That, Carlyn Ryklief

Inspiration 078: Focus on the Positives , Kaz Lock Clarke

Inspiration 079: 'I wouldn't miss this for the World', Eleisha McInnes

Inspiration 080: Forgive – Your Way to Success, Ruth Cyster-Stuettgen

Inspiration 081: Never Quit on a Bad Day, Dhea Bartlett

Inspiration 082: Make "You" your Number One Priority, Sue Ritchie

Inspiration 083: Gratitude

Inspiration 084: Be Your Biggest Accomplishment, Sara J Crawford

Inspiration 085: God Had a Plan for My Life, Ethelwynne Petersen

Inspiration 086: Honour Yourself – the Power of Now, Carla Trigo

Inspiration 087: Believe and You Will Achieve, Jenny Scott

Inspiration 088: Listen to Intuition, Rosemary O'Brien

Inspiration 089: Let Go of the Past, Michal Stewart

Inspiration 090: Forge Your Path, Bec Carroll-Bell

Inspiration 091: To the Girl in the Wings … , Kym Mulcahy

Inspiration 092: NOW is the Time!, Kim (Langtip) Wood

Inspiration 093: I am You, Mum, Emily Jones

Inspiration 094: Changes

Inspiration 095: Seek Happiness, Sara Maynard

Inspiration 096: The Art of Self Acceptance, Diana Bonwick

Inspiration 097: Remember, Beth Elaine Haynes

Inspiration 098: Seize the Day, Veena Vather

Inspiration 099: Give Thanks, Bianca Smith

Inspiration 100: My World Came Crumbling Down, Maureen Mbondiah Mandipaza

Inspiration 101: Unexpected Inspiration, Kathleen Buttigieg

Inspiration 102: Honour Your Body, Cathy Noël

Inspiration 103: You Can Do It!, Carol Carson

Inspiration 104: Zak, Leanne Woff

Inspiration 105: Friends are Everywhere, Lucy Johnson

Inspiration 106: Independent Mom, Cille Harris

Inspiration 107: "JUST", Jo Plummer

Inspiration 108: Reconnecting to the Goddess Within, Maria Jesus Romero (MariPosa)

Inspiration 109: Joy

Inspiration 110: My Paradise on This Earth, Leanne Swainson

Inspiration 111: My Challenges, My Inspiration, Mercy Mugure

Inspiration 112: OMG! It's About Me!, Kerry Upham

Inspiration 113: Embracing Change, Ingrid Stump

Inspiration 114: Step into the Extraordinary, Liesel Albrecht

Inspiration 115: Love is the Answer, Cheryl Campbell

Inspiration 116: Education Makes a Difference, Milka Roach

Inspiration 117: Love

Inspiration 118: Be Inspired by Change, Hazel Theocharous

Inspiration 119: Transformation Life by Design, Faye Waterman

Inspiration 120: Choices and My Mother, Natalya Stefanac

Inspiration 121: Fix Your Focus, Emily Farmer

Inspiration 122: You Are Resilient, Samara Egglezos

Inspiration 123: My Purpose

Inspiration 124: Now Choose Life, Cybelle Liporoni

Inspiration 125: Be Strong, Laura Stuettgen

Inspiration 126: I Love Myself, Melissa Groom

Inspiration 127: Autumn (Fall) Equinox, Emma Sidney

Inspiration 128: Old History, New History, Desiree Blaich

Inspiration 129: Let Your Feminine Empress Rise!, Jonita D'Souza

Inspiration 130: Letting Go

Inspiration 131: Be Yourself, Natalya Stefanac

Inspiration 132: For Life is a Journey, Susan Maslin

Inspiration 133: Have No Regrets, Katerina Egglezos

Inspiration 134: Are You Serious?, Sheridan Morris

Inspiration 135: Unfiltered Truth, Brenda Dempsey

Inspiration 136: What If?, Maike Sundmacher

Inspiration 137: Don't Quit, Tracey Hall

Inspiration 138: Inspiration

Inspiration 139: Finding Joy Through Grief, Vicki McClifty

Inspiration 140: Take Your Own Advice, Josie Kearsey

Inspiration 141: If You're a Daughter, Robyn Harrison

Inspiration 142: Hope and Intuition, Birgit Schwitalla

Inspiration 143: Focus

Inspiration 144: Flawsome Heroine, Ana Bogdanovska

Inspiration 145: Test Yourself, Farisai Dzemwa (Joymore)

Inspiration 146: Be ACE!, Heather Schmidt

Inspiration 147: Do What You Love, Melitta Hardenberg

Inspiration 148: I Am

Inspiration 149: Trust Yourself, Yukiko Mukumoto Ruthford

Inspiration 150: Sisters Since Six, Samantha Goss

Inspiration 151: Avoid Distraction and Focus on Action, Melanie Parker

Inspiration 152: Have High Standards, Rachpal Tulsi

Inspiration 153: Finding My Way, Joanne Golias

Inspiration 154: Blow Your Own Trumpet, Chris Dennis

Inspiration 155: Worthy Woman, Joanne Worthy

Inspiration 156: Find Your Voice, Rhonda Brown

Inspiration 157: Give and Be Blessed, Andrea Donaldson

Inspiration 158: Get Back Up!, Ritu Sharma

Inspiration 159: Everyone Has Their Own Story, Colleen Roberts

Inspiration 160: Hold True to Yourself, Linda Jabs

Inspiration 161: Do Less, Maria Paterakis

Inspiration 162: Cultivating Love, Shanti Clements

Inspiration 163: You CAN Do Anything, Shari Ware

Inspiration 164: Who is not good enough?, Iris Du

Inspiration 165: In Her Eyes, Bec Campbell

Inspiration 166: For Me

Inspiration 167: Touched by Faith, Luciane Sperling

Inspiration 168: True Beauty is in You, Jackie Wilson

Inspiration 169: From Broke to Abundant, Tracey Hall

Inspiration 170: Flow, Monika Miller

Inspiration 171: Finding Grace in Grief, Sandra Wallin

Inspiration 172: Simply Joy, Ruth Cyster-Stuettgen

Inspiration 173: Turning Points, Louise Plant

Inspiration 174: Equality, Alma Ram

Inspiration 175: Feminine Spirit Whisperings, Vicki Gotsis Ceraso

Inspiration 176: Break the Cycle, Kylie Farrugia

Inspiration 177: Self Worth, Zahia Araji

Inspiration 178: Celebrate

Inspiration 179: Embrace the "NOW", Nicole Maree Weatherley

Inspiration 180: It's About the 'Sparkle', Chris Georgopoulos

Inspiration 181: Let the True Journey Begin, Anita Ferrari

Inspiration 182: This Too Shall Pass, Karen Singery

Inspiration 183: Your Magical Life, Marion Hutton

Inspiration 184: Everything Happens For a Reason, Sharon Anderson

Inspiration 185: Embrace The Golden Muse in You, Chrisoula Sirigou

Inspiration 186: Connect with Your Heart, Fiona Craig

Inspiration 187: Dreams do Come True, Lani Sharp

Inspiration 188: Follow Your Purpose, Margaret Hiatt

Inspiration 189: Create Your Future, Adele Haussmann

Inspiration 190: The Joy of Style, Christine Maikousis

Inspiration 191: The Cycle of Inspiration, Christine Williams

Inspiration 192: Never Too Late, Benetta Wainman

Inspiration 193: Gratitude, Parents and Forgiveness, Desiree Blaich

Inspiration 194: Step into Your Greatness Queen, Maxine Palmer-Hunter

Inspiration 195: Is Fear Holding You Back?, Rosemary Teed

Inspiration 196: Touched by a Paw, Andrea Parascandalo

Inspiration 197: Random Act Of Kindness

Inspiration 198: Seize The Day, Bec Campbell

Inspiration 199: Winter Solstice, Emma Sidney

Inspiration 200: Some Advice, Levona Parker

Inspiration 201: Catharsis Through Writing, Jane Turner

Inspiration 202: You are Perfect, Margie O'Kane

Inspiration 203: Our Cries Reach Out, Juliet Okoye

Inspiration 204: Your Inner Truth, Josie Kearsey

Inspiration 205: All Answers Within, Brenda Dempsey

Inspiration 206: Lifestyle in Your Golden Years, Elaine Squiers

Inspiration 207: Your Story, Jacqui Hartley-Smith

Inspiration 208: Tantric Approach to Menopause, Jenni Mears

Inspiration 209: Do what Matters, Judy Mudie

Inspiration 210: Inspiration

Inspiration 211: Finding My 'Big Sister', Kimberley Bourgeois

Inspiration 212: Take Risks, Jo Johnson

Inspiration 213: The Rewards of Volunteering, Claire Sandell

Inspiration 214: Letting Go

Inspiration 215: Let it Happen, Isolde Martin

Inspiration 216: Find Inner Silence, Clarissa Hughes

Inspiration 217: Fire Within Me, Nisha Ukani

Inspiration 218: Jumping Roadblocks, Elaine Squiers

Inspiration 219: Who Am I Really?, Liesel Albrecht

Inspiration 220: Your Heart Longs To Sing!, Angi King

Inspiration 221: In the Name of Allah, Nida Mukhtar

Inspiration 222: You Are Loved, Karen Hooper

Inspiration 223: My Bucket List

Inspiration 224: Purposeful Living, Alice Ntobedzi

Inspiration 225: A Journey of Remembering, Beth Elaine Haynes

Inspiration 226: Seeing the Hidden Blessings, Leah Jade

Inspiration 227: It's About Perspective, Sharon Anderson

Inspiration 228: Your Soul Mate, Andrea Maynard-Brade

Inspiration 229: Love What You Do, Sharon Anderson

Inspiration 230: Let Me Love You Again, Bernie Giggins

Inspiration 231: Take Charge of Your Life, Dorcas Marimo

Inspiration 232: Invest in Yourself, Gaby Company

Inspiration 233: Allowing Truth, Marie Ireland

Inspiration 234: The Biggest Regrets in life, Rosie Shalhoub

Inspiration 235: Suffering in Silence Safiyah, Andrea Maynard-Brade

Inspiration 236: School, Khyrah Maynard-Ali

Inspiration 237: Dedication, Colleen Roberts

Inspiration 238: Mental Muscle, Rita Joyan

Inspiration 239: To Do What It Takes, Terry Bahat

Inspiration 240: An A-Z Manifesto, Pina Cerminara

Inspiration 241: Pursuit of Happiness, Andrea Parascandalo

Inspiration 242: Self Love

Inspiration 243: Be the Inspiration, Yvette Lazare

Inspiration 244: The Ripple Effect, Sarah Vitale

Inspiration 245: Eat Healthy, Dai Shaya Maynard-Gayle

Inspiration 246: Your Greatest Lesson, Emily Stuettgen

Inspiration 247: Shine Bright Like a Diamond, Rosie Shalhoub

Inspiration 248: I Focus On

Inspiration 249: Taking Care of You, Stephanie Wise

Inspiration 250: Paying it Forward, Stephanie Wise

Inspiration 251: I Focus On

Inspiration 252: Travel

Inspiration 253: I Focus On

Inspiration 254: A Lifelong Relationship, Renee Olsen

Inspiration 255: Follow Your Dreams, Rosine Ghantous

Inspiration 256: Take Time Out, Laura Stuettgen
Inspiration 257: Rise to Your Strength, Samara Egglezos
Inspiration 258: You Are Made to Impact, Emily Farmer
Inspiration 259: Make Friends with Your Money, Yvonne Morrison
Inspiration 260: Use Your POWER, Robyn Nelson
Inspiration 261: A Cat's Got Seven Lives, Rossana Fuentes
Inspiration 262: Let the Breeze Caress You, Anita Ferrari
Inspiration 263: Love, Joy and Peace, Luisa Russo
Inspiration 264: Affirmations
Inspiration 265: I Focus On
Inspiration 266: Step into Your Power!, Ali-P
Inspiration 267: Be Yourself, Uniquely You!, Maurissa Ailion
Inspiration 268: You Are One, Pip Ransome
Inspiration 269: Mind and Movement, Illona J Shooter
Inspiration 270: Choose the Way You Feel, Carolyn King
Inspiration 271: You Are, You Can, Carla Trigo
Inspiration 272: Happiness
Inspiration 273: Life – Don't Miss it!, Lyndie Jackson
Inspiration 274: Spring Equinox, Emma Sidney
Inspiration 275: Three H's, Karen Hooper
Inspiration 276: You are ENOUGH, Shani Suttie
Inspiration 277: Stop, Pray and Listen, Brenda Saunders/Todd
Inspiration 278: You Are What You Think, Georgina Bajer

Inspiration 279: No-one is Perfect, Ana Bogdanovska

Inspiration 280: Manifest Your Abundant Life, Tanya Rogers

Inspiration 281: Education

Inspiration 282: Am I Doing the Right Thing?, Leanne Woff

Inspiration 283: Curiously Simple Inspiration, Toni-Maree Hannan

Inspiration 284: Moments, Pauline M. Rohdich

Inspiration 285: Professional Bullying, Gameeda Henry

Inspiration 286: You are Destined to Succeed, Christy Amalu

Inspiration 287: Leap of Faith, Annie Toscher

Inspiration 288: I Focus On

Inspiration 289: Be of Service, Not Sacrifice, Helen Bolger-Harris

Inspiration 290: Inspiration

Inspiration 291: Resilience, Margaret Hiatt

Inspiration 292: Unleashing Your Inner Child, Brenda Dempsey

Inspiration 293: I Love Being 80!, Ethelwynne Petersen

Inspiration 294: I Focus On

Inspiration 295: A Well Woman – Getting it Right, Christy Amalu

Inspiration 296: It's Always the Darkest Before Dawn, Natalie Petersen

Inspiration 297: It's All About You, Ali Greer

Inspiration 298: A Celebration, Joanne Worthy

Inspiration 299: What makes a Mummy Like Me ..., Linda Reed-Enever

Inspiration 300: Yes, You Can, Grace Vassallo

Inspiration 301: Desire

Inspiration 302: Space Between Thoughts, Vanita Dahia

Inspiration 303: 'Go To India Where it All Began.', Margaret Hepworth

Inspiration 304: Touched by Recovery, Luciane Sperling

Inspiration 305: Life is a Piece of Cake!, Heather Belle Murphy

Inspiration 306: HOPE Will Never Fail You!, Jane Logue

Inspiration 307: The Sacred Goddess Promise, Maria Jesus Romero (MariPosa)

Inspiration 308: I Focus On

Inspiration 309: The Greatest Gift, Kerry Upham

Inspiration 310: Beautifully Broken, Ramona M. Pinckney

Inspiration 311: Beauty

Inspiration 312: Home, Monika Miller

Inspiration 313: Liberation, Helen Beeby

Inspiration 314: Let Go and Grow, Maxine Palmer-Hunter

Inspiration 315: We All Have Special Needs, Carlyn Ryklief

Inspiration 316: Flower by the Road, Marlene Richardt

Inspiration 317: Find Peace, Robyn Harrison

Inspiration 318: Wake up!, Rachel Gaia

Inspiration 319: Good Impressions, Aylee Sunstrom

Inspiration 320: True Mirror, Ana Bogdanovska

Inspiration 321: You Matter, Glyn Conlon

Inspiration 322: Gratitude Dinners, Rosemary Teed

Inspiration 323: Inspiration

Inspiration 324: Tenacity, Lisa Sweeney

Inspiration 325: Success is Personal, Tracey Maclay

Inspiration 326: Admire and Inspire, Kristie Dean

Inspiration 327: Embrace New Chapters, Janet McNeill

Inspiration 328: The Chameleon, Maxine Palmer-Hunter

Inspiration 329: Have Courage, Jacinda McIntosh

Inspiration 330: Be the Lighthouse, Melissa Groom

Inspiration 331: Transformation from Childhood, Katerina Egglezos

Inspiration 332: Listen to Your Heart, Jo Schutt

Inspiration 333: Intention

Inspiration 334: Embracing Change, Joanne Whalen

Inspiration 335: No Regrets, Christy Amalu

Inspiration 336: Allow Grief, Debbie Singh

Inspiration 337: Ten Things, Natasa Denman

Inspiration 338: Change Comparison Into Inspiration, Miranda Powell

Inspiration 339: Syrian Refugees, Cille Harris

Inspiration 340: Today and Tomorrow, Monika Miller

Inspiration 341: Choose to be Strong, Carla Fogazzi

Inspiration 342: Sheer Persistence, Faye Waterman

Inspiration 343: Reflect

Inspiration 344: Second Chance, Melissa Griffiths

Inspiration 345: The Undiscovered, Virginia Phillips

Inspiration 346: Listen to Feedback, Christina Sanchez

Inspiration 347: Embrace Pathways, Hazel Theocharous

Inspiration 348: The Power of Persistence, Andrea Donaldson

Inspiration 349: You Are Your Own Destiny, Neenah Olivier-Stewart

Inspiration 350: Your Suffering is Your Gift!, Lillian Benrubi

Inspiration 351: The Power Of The Dream, Piera-Angela Bottari

Inspiration 352

Inspiration 353: Small Daily Activities, Linda Clucas

Inspiration 354: Family Life and Obstacles, Merlene Crossfield

Inspiration 355: Perfect Peaches, Lisa Linton

Inspiration 356: I Focus On

Inspiration 357: Take Your Own Path, Joelle Wörtche

Inspiration 358: I am…, Eleni Ikon

Inspiration 359: Dream, Christine Stow

Inspiration 360: Reflections, Michal Stewart

Inspiration 361: A Real Woman, Gina Collins

Inspiration 362: The Infinite Joy of Being YOU, Shivany Gonell

Inspiration 363: "Hey, You! Yeah, You!", Laura Abrams

Inspiration 364: The Unexpected Experience, Zynoe Bayat Abrahams

Inspiration 365

Introduction

Words spoken with love can change your life in an instant.

With our words of encouragement in "The Book of Inspiration for Women by Women", we are giving you a gentle nudge, a timely reminder to get you out of your comfort zone and make changes to your life.

Women are naturally courageous, strong and powerful. Sometimes through their pain and challenges they lose focus. By sharing our messages of wisdom in this book we are sending you a big, loving hug, a gentle and re-assuring hand squeeze.

If you're holding this book in your hand it is right for you; you are meant to read it. You may not know why, just be okay with that. If you have been searching for answers, suffering, struggling, stuck and not known which way to turn, you are bound to find the answers here.

Allow the wisdom within these pages to help heal the brokenness deep within you, keep your hopes up, to uplift and encourage you, to help you rise up and to stay on top.

The intention of this book is to bring back happiness and laughter into your life.

Every single one of us needs some kind of support at some stage in our life. The women and the girls in this book are here to support you each and every day. Working on our inner-self is a journey, believe deeply that you were meant to be here now, and keep the big vision in mind.

It is with great honour and humbleness that I present to you the authors who have gifted you their wisdom and words to allow you to feel supported. It is my vision that through these pages you will be encouraged to go deep within and discover your purpose and your power.

Allow the inspiration to be forthcoming from you as well as you are part of this special gift to the world. Allow the pages to speak to you. Feel encouraged to pick up the pen and create your message of inspiration on the pages provided. You have the opportunity to reflect and create your life as you wish it to be.

The Book is as much yours as it is ours. Let's make a difference in each of our corners of the world. Let's make it a better place, for each and everyone, especially for those girls that are growing into future women of the world. Let's collectively pass the baton of wisdom and feminine power on to these beautiful young souls.

with Love and Inspiration, Ruth Cyster-Stuettgen
April 2017

Inspiration 001

Just Breathe

Nisha Ukani

To start with, take a deep breath. I would love to share a thought of a little girl who is still in a woman. The inspiration you seek is already within your soul, evolving into a higher self of connecting to God. As a little girl I always felt happy, helping others. My secret was simple: 'I pray'. As I join my hands and bow my head I always pray 'Send the right person at the right time with hope and belief.'

A little girl kept on telling me 'there is always a way'. With this attitude in my life, I have come a long way with a kind heart, brave spirit and beautiful mind. As the time flies, ups and downs come along but never shatter me. Be grounded to your roots for how you are created, your optimistic faith will lead you to the path of achievement. One's soul is healed and purified by being with the child within you. So love yourself and your investments will never go wrong. Train your mind to see good in every situation life brings.

A mantra that raises your inner peace and brings out love and care is to be grateful for everything.

Namaste.

Nisha Ukani is an Artist, Jewellery Designer and Hairstylist from Melbourne Australia

Inspiration 002

You are Enough

Sarah Huon

We spend our lives as women thinking we have to work harder, stay later, constantly proving ourself to others to show that we are worth it. What makes us worthy? What makes us believe in ourselves?

I believe in surrounding myself with positive people, people who are able to lift me up and give me encouragement and support whenever I need it. I know that there are times in my life when I have wanted to give up, to hide and give in to the pressures of the day, the hour, the minute and to cry and fall apart. I've been unemployed, lost my business, had no money for groceries, been married and divorced three times, had my first born child endure open heart surgery at 12 weeks old. There are always moments in our lives that test us and push us to our limits, but I honestly believe that there are people out there who are so much worse off.

Surround yourself in affirmations, positive messages, vision boards, a place of peace and retreat, people who fill your cup with love and support and distance yourself from negativity. Join a women's networking group that wraps its arms around you and nurtures you. Get outdoors and exercise. Have coffee with girlfriends. Be honest and true and love will follow, and don't forget, you are enough.

Sarah Huon is a Finance Broker, Entrepreneur from Melbourne, Australia

Inspiration 003

Summer Solstice

Emma Sidney

In the Southern Hemisphere, we are preparing for Christmas (see the Winter Solstice for traditional celebrations). Because it's hot, many ditch the turkey and ham in favour of salads and chicken, prawns or vegetarian dishes. As we near our holiday season this day can be unconsciously overlooked and unjustly so. For here we can reflect on our successes, how the year went, how our dreams and goals became reality.

This moment has long been celebrated as Litha or Vestalia and in the UK people still flock to Stonehenge to see the sun rise on this long day (in June of course).

Walk along a beach or river, listen to the water and feel the grace of the earth between your toes. Write down how your world is at this time, feel the flow of the light through your days and as the weather heats up even more find time to relax and enjoy the balm of heat and light.

What will you change? What felt right? With a new year ahead, there's much to do and be. It's almost the new year, jump start those new goals and dreams!

Emma Sidney is a Business Owner, Copywriter from Melbourne, Australia

Inspiration 004

You are Destined to Succeed

Christy Amalu

Christy was born in rural Africa after a civil war. She was meant to have been born with a silver spoon in her mouth as both parents were educated and gainfully employed before the war but there was famine at the time and war had left people empowerished. She subsequently lost her Dad at the age of five, was raised by her Mum with her other five siblings. Her childhood experience and the challenges she passed through in life were enough to stop her but she believes, never says that she cannot do anything, or that anything seems impossible, no matter how discouraging or harrowing that situation may be; we are limited only by what we allow ourselves to be limited by: that's our own minds.

We are the masters of our own reality; and when we become self-aware to this fact; absolutely anything in the world is possible. Master yourself, and become king of the world around you. Let no odds, chastisement, exile, doubt, fear or hatred, prevent you from achieving your dreams. Never be a victim of life; be a conqueror. Note: any circumstance surrounding you at the moment is subject to change. I am encouraging you to keep your head high and don't give up.

*Christy Amalu is a Clinical Nurse Advisor
from Milton Keynes, UK*

Inspiration 005

You are Wise

Diana Rickman

I used to charge through life in a super hero suit. Fixing, organising and making everyone else happy not daring to look up and think about what I really wanted. Then I became depressed. Not that I would have admitted it to you! I had compassion for other people's weakness but not my own!

By chance I learned about Emotional Freedom Technique. I couldn't believe that something so simple and strange could have such a amazing effect. In spite of my doubts EFT fascinated me and I began to learn and use the technique. Beliefs and habits quickly disappeared and I began to love and accept myself just as I am.

Using EFT I felt brave enough to express myself authentically and calm enough to hear my own wisdom.

- You don't need to be a super hero to change your life.
- Accept and love your weakness. It's where your compassion comes from.
- You are wise. This may take time to accept but you know yourself best.
- You are enough.

Diana Rickman is an EFT Practitioner and Mindset Coach from Hastings, New Zealand

Inspiration 006

Self Worth

April Livingstone

'Your self-worth is determined by you. You don't have to depend on someone telling you who you are.'
– Beyoncé

I like this quote because it helps to provide people with a sense of self worth. It helps us to remember that we are our own person and do not need to depend on others to feel good in ourselves.

I find this inspirational as I feel it is important to realise that we should feel good inside our own skin without the judgement of those around us.

April Livingstone is a student from Melbourne, Australia

Inspiration 007

Honour Family

Emily Stuettgen

For my entire life, I have had the incredible privilege to be surrounded by strong, independent, beautiful women. The effect of their confidence has encouraged me from a young age to be comfortable in my own way. To have the opportunity to lean on your family is such an incredible gift, and I am grateful beyond words. Even now, I can see how I have been moulded by the women who have helped raise me into who I am today. From learning to be generous, like Carol, and gentle like Pearl, good-humoured like June, witty like Edith and resilient like Ruth, I can safely say that my grandmother, Lorraine, raised these women right, and they in turn have helped me grow into who I am. It is so important to me to maintain these simple yet meaningful memories as I am certain that I will do everything I can to pass these traits on to my children in the future.

I may have doubts about what the future holds, but I know I can always count on my family to guide me, and I hold them close to my heart.

Emily Stuettgen is a Student from Melbourne, Australia

Inspiration 008

Something Inside so Strong

Andrea Maynard-Brade

After surviving 13 years in an abusive relationship, I felt my dreams of running my own business were shattered by being battered. I thought my life was limited to what I could achieve, I thought I had to be realistic, logical, practical, with no dreams, desires or purpose to live for.

I stopped blaming someone for my pain, took responsibility for my own actions and my worth and moved away from people who held me back, people who were not allowing me to fulfil my dreams and potential. I needed to find my inner self, my now, my love, my light and my life.

I urge you to be authentic, be transparent about what you are protecting, defending and hiding, your inner spirit will awaken and your mindset will change from being a victim to victorious. Only then will your realignment with your true purpose in life start manifesting.

So follow your heart, dreams, destiny by honouring thyself with integrity, love and light and become a nurture of the universe and transform lives.

Blissing in Abundance Beautiful Queens.

Andrea Maynard-Brade is a Master Health Coach, Author, Speaker, Holistic Therapist and Director from Walsall, United Kingdom

Inspiration 009

Differences

Natasha Hogan

A recipe for a baby!

The six basic needs

<u>Ingredients : -</u>
- Eat a balanced diet - Not a fashionable diet... everything in moderation and tweak it to any conditions.

<u>Method: -</u>
- Love Yourself - it is a strength, not a weakness.
- Be Gentle & Kind - it will serve you well.
- Water Often - like a flower, hydrate, hydrate, hydrate - keep our skin & cells supple.

<u>Bake: -</u>
- With Exercise - Our bodies still need to move, and not the kind of crazy busy running around we often do.

<u>Time: -</u>
- Minimum 20minutes a day - Meditate and or do, what it is, that calms and relaxes you.

The Ultimate Want - To be happy & fulfilled in our own selves.

A baby

Natasha Hogan is a Mummychiever & Author from Mareeba, Queensland, Australia

Inspiration 010

Just Because I am a Daughter...

Ritu Sharma

She was born a girl. So she was placed in a corner. She grew in the nook of a fully blossomed garden. She was under-nourished but her roots were adamant to support her and build her up. Deprived of love, she still learnt to smile because it felt great. Her height and spread were controlled according to the gardener's wishes. She would occasionally try and bend to admire and connect to her roots. The gardener disliked that.

After a while, she was removed and replanted. It was a different garden with lesser fertilisers and water. However, as nature would allow, the sun would shine, the wind would blow and the rain would come down. She continued to grow. The weeds around her tried to pull her down while the parasites endeavoured to engulf her. She was determined to live on. Her strength was too huge. She had grown spikes over time for defence. She produced the sweetest of fruits and she was, yet, the most beautiful flower in the garden.

Lots of love to all daughters!

*Ritu Sharma is a Teacher,
Inspirational Speaker and Entrepreneur
from Walsall, England*

Inspiration 011

Dream

What are my big dreams?

What is one thing I can do today toward achieving my dream?

Inspiration 012

Touched by Crisis

Luciane Sperling

When crisis rises in your life no matter how much you may try to avoid it, it will usually show as unwanted experiences that take us out of inner peace and comfort zones. Typically crisis result in some level of loss, but also can bring growth, forcing change.

Believe you won't be confronted with crises you can't handle. Trees stand strong because of the wind; no person can be strong without a challenge. Be thankful for yours.

Face your challenges, find your blessings, grow from there, and change your world to what you really want.

In order to face any challenge, try to focus specifically on the positive result:

> F – Faith in what you want to achieve will keep your vision inspired on the positive.
> O – Out coming results based on your attitude and ability to visualize your expectation.
> C – Connections through effective and pro-active communications with community.
> U – Uniform, be constant, stable and consistent in your decisions.
> S – Safe, whatever you do, do it in a safe way.

Luciane Sperling is an Author, Inspirational Speaker and Global Entrepreneur from Sydney, Australia

Inspiration 013

What is Love, Anyway?

Maddison Ellerton

There are many things that I have learnt through the short 17 years of my life, but the one thing that has stood out the most is Love. But why love? What is so special about it? Is it the way it makes you feel, the butterflies or the first date? Why is it so important? Why does everybody crave to be in love?

I don't know but much about love, but what I do know, is that love can change the world. If we spread love and positivity throughout our lives, within ourselves and others, we can make the world a happier place, with less harm, abuse, fighting and anger. Our generation can change the way we view things, the way we see other people and the way we live our own lives.

Love is so painful, but if we as a community send not only love but positivity, kindness and encouragements, the world can be a magical place.

Maddison Ellerton is a Student from Melbourne, Australia

Inspiration 014

The Power of Prayer

Dr Linet Amalie

It doesn't matter what religion or faith you belong to. Prayer, or positive thoughts you send to others is powerful because it comes from within your soul and the intent and meaning behind it is where the power lies. To have positive regard and intention to help others by way of healing, and then send it to another by thought, is what I would classify as the basis of prayer.

Positive thoughts for healing, or to give heartfelt thanks for what you have received, is, in my view, a genuine and honest connection between your soul and theirs. The intent to send love and blessings to another person, place, animal or structure, to ensure that whatever situation surrounds them at that point in time is sent with love and purity of thought: this is what connects you with them, and connection is what is important. There is no right or wrong in prayer. It is extremely personal to YOU and no one else. Each and every religion or faith will pray in their own unique way and as long as you believe in this, and I mean REALLY believe at a deep soul level, then your prayers will be heard.

Dr Linet Amalie is a Medium, Author and Educator from Melbourne, Australia

Inspiration 015

Find Your "Why"

Shari Ware

When it comes to achieving any goal in life that you have set for yourself, THE most important key to your success or failure is the power of your WHY. The easiest way to explain it is with a quote from a book called *The Secret Code of Success* by Noah St John: "You can't fix a why to problem with a how to answer." I will use weight loss as an example. What this means is that we all know HOW to lose weight don't we? We know that we need to eat better and ideally move more. So why don't we do it? If we don't, it's because our whys are not strong enough and quite often it is also because our why nots are actually stronger.

We all have reasons why we want to do certain things and reasons why we don't want to. If we want to be successful at anything, then our whys need to be stronger than our why nots. Find your "Why Power" and you will be successful at anything that you set out to do!

Shari Ware is a Weightloss Mindset Mentor from Brisbane, Australia

Inspiration 016

Sisterhood

Carol Ray

"It's about women helping women and women doing things together and supporting each other."
– Diana Burch

There's something innately unique about women's relationships with other women, and in particular, those who share the joys and despairs of motherhood. In my short journey with Mumma Bears, I have been overwhelmed by the women in our community willingly giving of their time, experience and love. Amongst the growing cynicism of the world, are many truly remarkable, yet unrecognised women walking amongst us.

They are not the curers of cancer or the recipients of the Noble Prize, but women who have overcome adversity and are now strong enough to mentor and empower others. I have met many of these women – those who have been abused by an ex partner, lost a child or parent, endured teenage pregnancy, overcome addiction or been ostracised by their family. Their inner fortitude is a force to be reckoned with and rather than choosing to live their lives forever the victim, they have consciously chosen to move onwards and upwards and leave their adversities behind. They take their experience and use it to make them a more understanding, empathetic and resilient person. MUMMA BEARS' women inspire me!

*Carol Ray is a Teacher and Mumma Bears Founder
from Melbourne, Australia*

Inspiration 017

Distinction Takes Time

Suzanne Johnson

Success doesn't mean it was always that way. Hardship and adversity gave me the motivation, understanding and personal skills that were required to make this journey in Beauty Therapy.

In my late twenties my three sons needed support. Working fulltime didn't provide adequate income. So what was I truly interested in? What would I be happy to do for a lifetime? Beauty Therapy was the answer because it demands challenging practical and social skills. A redundancy package from my then employer wasn't enough, so the car was sold and we walked everywhere. To begin the new career the alarm was set for two each morning to study. A lot can be achieved when a household is sleeping. Time passed, and so did I, with high distinction!

Every week an income became more pressing. Jubilation – an agent called, the local newspaper was vacating its premises. Although too large for my requirements and too expensive, I took the risk. Peaches & Cream was born. Today, three workplaces and three decades later, hundreds of women have confided their stories to me, a rich education. Still enjoying this chosen field, my role has expanded to include Director, Educator and co-Author.

Suzanne Johnson has a Bachelor of Health Science – Dermal Therapies from Melbourne, Australia

Inspiration 018

The Pursuit of Authenticity

Vicki McClifty

Practice tuning into your emotions and dealing with them, rather than avoiding the pain. Emotions are the barometer to your soul's purpose. By burying negative emotions, you become stuck, get depressed and anxious. Consequently, finding your purpose and vision becomes a struggle. It is only when you experience and question your emotions that you discover the real You. Peeling back the layers you uncover your strengths and passions. You tune into your heart and follow your intuition, in lieu of following others. You discover your own authentic power. This is your path to personal freedom.

Choose to create a safe and supportive environment to share your stories and lighten your burden. This is essential to healing. Make your world a haven where time is allocated to care for each other and yourself. This process will transform your life to one where dreams are pursued and trust is re-established. Where truth is infinite.

We are authentic souls sharing this life experience. Let us learn to nurture the gift that is life. This gift which brings us all the freedom to explore fearlessly and ultimately brings us joy.

Vicki McClifty is a Life Enhancement Coach and host of AM Healing My Soul from Brisbane, Australia

Inspiration 019

No Wound Too Great

Deb Ware

Inspiration is conquering the things we don't think we can achieve, it's facing our darkest fears and believing in the unbelievable, all to then help others.

We all have scars. I believed that the scars from my past would remain open wounds dictating the outcome of my future. When I stopped this negative thinking, when I found my purpose in life, of who God created me to be, it turned my wounds into moments to help, inspire, influence and bring life to others.

I began to put my hand out to help children from difficult backgrounds, have compassion for those who are depressed, make meals for those who mourn, be a motivating voice to women in prison, to run fundraisers to raise money for the poor and speak truth of beauty in girls with eating disorders. We all need to be reminded that we can conquer anything. We are beautiful, we are loved and we are all extraordinarily gifted.

Joshua 1:7 – *Be strong and courageous. Do not be afraid; do not be discouraged, for the Lord your God will be with you wherever you go.*

*Deb Ware is a Carer/Charity Worker
from Melbourne, Australia*

Inspiration 020

Feelings

What am I feeling now?

What do I notice about myself?

What will I do to feel the way I want to feel?

Inspiration 021

You Too Can Survive

Maxine Harris-Burton

He was manipulative, controlling and demanded all my time and attention, yet I survived. He made me doubt my abilities and tried to stop me extending my education and training, yet I survived. He claimed he loved me with all his heart yet accused me of sleeping with his best friend and went off with my now ex-best friend, yet I survived.

He would take me to lovely places, buy me gifts and write me beautiful love poems, yet I survived. He once took another girl out to meet his friends behind my back, yet I survived. He drove me to an isolated dark lonely place and threatened to kill me, yet I survived.

I was young and naive and did not know this was domestic abuse as he had never hit me. I learned that emotional abuse could be as powerful as a punch in the face, yet I survived because I had a strong supportive friend who helped me get out of that relationship. I am now a director of my own company.

All women going through a similar thing, be strong because you too can survive!

Maxine Harris-Burton is a Director, Social Care Company from West Midlands UK

Inspiration 022

To My Sisters With Love

Emma Sidney

You who began as a fragile beauty, a bundle of chubby hand-holding, cuddles and sweetness. You have within you the far reaches of the universe. To conceive, to love, raise and protect. Your arms encompassing, warm as the sun. Welcome sister. Join me in offering love to all, be unique and also One.

One spirit of sensual, sweet desire, that lifts mankind higher and higher.

One shining light to forge the way. Guiding men to care as they play.

One sisterhood in global knowing. Of nurturing, joyful, play and growing.

Within you lies both spark and forest fire. A river of excitement and wellspring of tenderness. A soft Summer breeze and Arctic gale. Endless caverns and the awe of the Grand Canyon.

You are sacred an expression of the divine. You are the sun through which we all are born. Sometimes, I know my love, you feel small. But without you mankind is nothing at all.

So lift your head sweetheart, join us here. Rejoice and know your sisters are near.

Emma Sidney is a Digital Copywriter and Inspirational Speaker from Melbourne, Australia

Inspiration 023

Be a Queen

Desh Dixon

A Queen: Royal and Immaculate, Educates and Empowers, Perfectly, Herself.

Dear Queen, stand in your magnificence. You are a perfectly imperfect beautiful creation of God. You have no idea how loved you are, how powerful you are, how incredible you are, just as you are. You are enough! Life happens to all of us. No matter your past mistakes, you are and will always be a Queen. Look in the mirror and admire the godd*mn reflection!

Queens do not settle. When it comes to a relationships, do not settle! You deserve to be with someone who honours you. A Queen is only fit for a true King. Do not rush the process. Single is not a disease. When the time is right, I believe you and your King will come together. So in the meantime, invest in yourself. Give more to yourself. Love yourself. Treat yourself. Live your life. Get back to your dreams. Do what makes you happy. Travel the world. Move to a new city. Increase your self-confidence. Increase your self-love. Focus on YOU. YOU are way too REGAL to accept anything less than the best! Period! And you must never forget that.

Desh Dixon is an Author, Poet and Speaker from Washington DC, USA

Inspiration 024

Trust the Road Less Traveled

Stacie Coleman

"You either walk inside your story and own it, or you walk outside your story & hustle for your worthiness."
– Brené Brown

Sometimes all you have to go on is your own inner knowing and a whole lot of faith. No matter where you came from, no matter where you're at now, trust that subtle voice inside of your head. I like to think of it as 'GOD'S VOICE' and it's there to guide you.

Let go of past mistakes and embrace the ones to come, because they will. But this is where you'll grow. This is where you'll learn who you truly are and exactly what you're made of.

Not everyone will understand, and sometimes especially those closest to you. That's okay. Don't try to convince or prove yourself to anyone. DO however, trade in your wishbone for a backbone and STAND behind your beliefs 100%. GOD has already given you everything you need. Trust within, NEVER give up, and stay persistent. Go after your true calling and the big dreams you have in your heart. You're worth it!

Stacie Coleman is a Speaker, Author and Child Confidence Coach from Burlington, United States

Inspiration 025

Bubbles

Gameeda Henry

Effervescent, energetic, light
See through, honest and open
Reflecting all the colours of the rainbow
Surrounded with fun and laughter
Have exceptional resilience and buoyancy
Achieve great heights and are highly successful

Do not mix with dark, murky substances
Have no hidden agendas or false facades
No bushels under which to hide their light
Negativity and criticism can't stem their enthusiasm
Get sometimes pricked by thorns
But don't bear any grudges or carry burdens

Make time and space for others
Give sound advice when asked
Share their expertise and flop-proof recipes
Set goals and tackle tasks head-on
Think things through and plan ahead
Never elope or shirk responsibilities

Bubbles are up-beat and positive
Get things done with realistic time-frames
Have more ups than downs
Always surface when thrown into the deep end
Cherish friendships and have good intrinsic values
Survive life's onslaughts with their souls intact!

To my sister Marlene for surviving in the workplace
With love: Gameeda
(12 November 2012)

*Gameeda Henry is a Teacher
from Stellenbosch, South Africa*

Inspiration 026

Intentions to Fly

Mel Williams

How often do you feel stuck or fearful as though you cannot move forward? Have negative, disempowering thoughts and think "what's the right decision?" At some stage in our lives, we all do, it seems human nature to do so. This is because we have been conditioned by others to think this way. When we were born we had none of these thought processes. We were born with love thoughts only – no stress and no fear.

It is possible to leave those conditioned thoughts behind because anything is possible! Grab, hold tight to an intention. Don't make it a wish. Set it in your mind, write it down. Make that thought, that desire a real picture in your head. Set your intention, follow its path, be committed, live fearlessly, taking every piece that shows up to play for you.

Setting your intenion and picturing it in your mind is a very powerful motivator. Nothing I have achieved was by simple luck or right place, right time. It is because I intended it that way.

No one plays your drum like you. So set your path through the power of your own mind – Your Intentions!

Mel Williams is a Founder, Director, CEO and Business Mentor, from Eurobin, Victoria, Australia

Inspiration 027

Life is Painful, Suffering is Optional

Marg Lange

"You're so sensitive," said Mother. "You're lazy," said Grandmother. "You're so vain," said a sister. "You look like a tart when you wear red lipstick," said another sister. "You got it easy," said another sister in relation to our domestic violent upbringing. "If the miscarriage didn't happen and the boy survived you wouldn't have been born," said Father.

The story of my false identity was set. By age eight we are sponges to all that we are hear and see. I took lack of self-worth, self-esteem, guilt and shame into every aspect of my life. I sucked it up, worked like a dog, and carried the expectation of rejection and abandonment at every relationship, be it personal or professional, and suffered. Recognising the negative stories you've been telling yourself that formulate your belief systems of who you are, is the end to the suffering. Life will serve you up painful gifts to give you the required experiences to grow. Reframe each experience as if you were a movie director observing each experience. Ask yourself, "What did I miss?" This is where the truth lies. The power to change your story is the beginning to living your life authentically.

Marg Lange is a Small Business Owner from Melbourne, Australia

Pay it Forward

Jerry Penny

I have always embraced the 'pay it forward' revolution, for long before it became a term or a trend. I remember one Boxing Day walking around my town offering my collection of toys. Why? Because someone told me that Boxing Day was the day to give away what you didn't need anymore. Since then, I have always felt the need to always do my best to help others in need, even if it's just a smile. It's amazing what you attract when you are in this frame of mind, and you start to attract people who need help.

Are you doing the same in life and business? Some business owners think it's enough to have a transaction-based relationship with their customers. Don't forget the most important message, whether it's in personal or business relationships, is that appreciation matters! Appreciate and be grateful for everyone in your life, and make sure you remember to make the effort to thank and acknowledge those people.

Jerry Penny is a Relationship Marketing Coach and Direct Sales Trainer from Melbourne, Australia

Inspiration 029

Get Out of Your Head and Back Into Your Gut

Marylin Schirmer

You ARE good enough! You are NOT going crazy! It's just a lack of education that no one's been teaching, until now that is.

Women are not meant to be so much in our 'head' or use our 'heart' for decision making, if it's out of alignment with our gut instinct. We've ended up valuing logic (the male brain GPS) over our female instinct (the female GPS).

Anything that teaches women to be consistent in behaviour is based on the premise that we have a male brain. Monthly hormonal fluctuations effect different brain area functions at different times of the month which in no way makes us stupid, we just need to use our gut instinct more often, which is even more effective for us.

Women are like iPhone hardware devices and men are like android hardware devices. What happens if you try to run android apps in an iPhone? Frazzled! Accept your exquisite design completely and even love and thank it. For without it there would be no people on the planet.

Foggy brain just means you don't have to think and hand over to your gut instinct instead. We are NOT complicated, just uninformed.

Marylin Schirmer is a specialist in the psychology of Womens Issues from Brisbane, Australia

Inspiration 030

Be Yourself

Blaise van Hecke

We are conditioned to run with the pack, be like everyone else in order to fit in. There is a duality to this because we are all unique. By fitting in to be accepted means that we must compromise who we really are. Who wants to be the same as everyone else anyway? The people who are most successful and happy are those who have found their authenticity and lived life to their own rules.

It's not easy. For myself, it was always much easier to go under the radar, not make waves and then I found myself bursting to get out. My real self. As I approach my fiftieth year, I find that my actions and words are more true to myself. People around me possibly think that I am going through a midlife crisis but I am actually getting back to me.

And guess what? Your real self is pretty damn good. Not that clone of 'everyone else' but someone with ideas and thoughts that are useful to the world. It's a very satisfying place to be.

Blaise van Hecke is an award-winning Writer and Publisher, from Melbourne, Australia

Inspiration 031

Be The Boss of Your Life

Tekka-Lee Williams

Have you ever been pushed around by bullies, been called names? Well those people are simply just jealous of you. It took me sometime to realise this fact.

So I decided to take my stand against those people by ignoring them and focused my thoughts on the positives within my life. I came to realise that the more positive thoughts I had, the happier I became.

I am now moving forward in my life because I've chosen a positive mindset and now I have the life I want.

You too can have the life YOU want by changing your thoughts, and you will then go further than the stars!

Be the Boss of Your Life!

Tekka-Lee Williams is a Business Owner and Primary School Student from Eurobin, Victoria, Australia

Inspiration 032

Inspiration

What has inspired me today?

Who has inspired me today?

Whom have I inspired today?

Inspiration 033

Self Love

Margaret Ioannidis

Looking within was never easy for me! The last 15 years I have worked on so much of my inner muse, soul and love for self, that today I feel complete and at one with myself. At times when there is a trauma it changes you. I didn't fit in as a child anywhere, was used, abused, lost my parents in my early 20's, took drugs and was outcast by family seeing me as the selfish one. But I met my soulmate.

My first child almost died, I had two more children and have followed my passion and purpose as a healer – helping woman, holding red tents – it all makes you look within. Attracting great women, friends and changing relationships. What counts more than anything is Life. My life. My love, my purpose. My family. I know that when there is self love, constant focus and love. I totally believe that within us all we have a story to love and embrace. Look in the mirror and love all of you. You are perfect and complete. Show the world who you are! You have everything to gain. You're worth it.

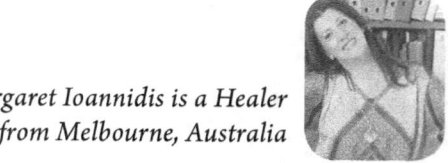

*Margaret Ioannidis is a Healer
from Melbourne, Australia*

Inspiration 034

Contemplation

Roz Tilley

Where do you find Inspiration? Not on any street corner. Look into your own heart. You may feel it comes from somewhere else. "Oh, if I have a partner I will be happy." "If I have money it will make a difference." You achieve these things and you observe yourself, and something is still missing.

When you can find peace deep within your core you will honour yourself and the energy that you have created. Don't give people permission to make you feel less than you are, and, in turn, they cannot make you feel any emotion you don't wish to feel. The responsibility is all yours. Search your emotions and find out what you require for your personal growth. Find peace with yourself, this may not come easily. Be aware but not critical of others, you have no idea where their path takes them. You cannot walk in anyone else's shoes. Be gentle with yourself, it is your unique journey. Look at what Mother Earth and Nature have provided. When you can see the magic of Nature, honour her finery and understand the wisdom of the Earth, then you are ready to find your personal peace in contemplation.

Roz Tilley is an Author, Illustrator and specialises in Healing. Roz is from the Yarra Valley, Australia.

Inspiration 035

Going Deeper...

Jutta Maria Hecht

"I want to go deeper."

This is what came out when I was asked by one of my teachers what I wanted. This happened over twenty-five years ago in India after I left my very successful, fast paced business life in Germany. Even though it looked from the outside that I 'had it all' I felt empty inside. My inner journey began. Going deeper, learning to listen with new ears, seeing with new eyes, feeling into my self and reintegrating my whole being from the inside out.

Cultivating these new skills required me really slowing down, time to be with myself in a truly loving and nurturing way. Every morning became a ritual in ayurvedic practices to nourish my body and mind, providing a stable foundation for my day. Giving myself a warm oil massage and using my breath in meditation to become more clear. I started to align with nature again, with her rhythms and elements, deeply embracing that I am part of nature and nature is part of me. Going deeper... into my wise and wild nature as a woman, living more and more from this deeply rooted, flowing force from within. Going deeper...

Jutta Maria Hecht is an Ayurvedic Holistic Spiritual Practitioner and Mentor from Encinitas, USA

Inspiration 036

No Compromises

Laura Stuettgen

"If you just set out to be liked, you would be prepared to compromise on anything at any time, and you would achieve nothing."
– Margaret Thatcher

An important lesson I have learnt over time, is that you cannot please everyone in life. If I did, I would be wasting my time and precious energy. There will always be people who do not agree with what I stand for or what I do. If I stopped and doubted myself when I hear their opinions against me, I would never achieve those things that I believe are important to me. Be brave and confident to stand up for what you believe in – do not compromise.

Be unapologetic and unwavering in your faith and belief, regardless of whether you are liked or not. You can achieve anything you set your mind to. Disregard the naysayers.

Laura Stuettgen is a Recruitment Consultant from Melbourne, Australia

Inspiration 037

Be Your Best

Georgia Van Der Poel

When I was little my mum and dad always told me to try my best at everything. Even if I didn't succeed the first time I would try and try again. My mum always tells me the "R" in my name stands for relentless.

Be your best, put it to the test, because you'll never know, 'till you have a go!

Beautiful ~ Extraordinary

Yourself ~ Original ~ Unique ~ Real

Brilliant ~ Elegant ~ Spontaneous ~ Terrific

Georgia Van Der Poel is a Student from Melbourne, Australia

Inspiration 038

Never Give Up

Emily Buckley-Fourter

My name is Emily and this is my story. I am 21 years of age and I have a disability. I have been doing a transition to employment program for the past three years, to help prepare me for getting a job. I have been prepared to try all sorts of work in the hope I find a job. My perseverance has paid off. I now have a paid job at Coles and I also volunteer at an Opportunity shop and the local library. I am doing work experience at a cafe. I received an award at Coles for making both the team and the customers smile. I was so proud to be told that my presence creates an energetic culture and that I am an asset to the team.

I like all of the work I do because I get to help people which makes me happy and to learn new skills. I really enjoy my volunteer work. I hope I inspire other people with a disability to believe that they too can get a job and to never give up.

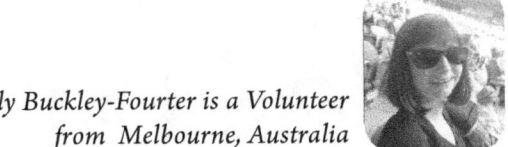

Emily Buckley-Fourter is a Volunteer from Melbourne, Australia

Inspiration 039

Mind Matters

Vanita Dahia

Women are resilient and steadfast in their domestic and work life. Women cope and strategically weave in the loving kindness and tenderness to sooth the hurt and warm the heart of their child or loved ones. She uses skilful reflection balancing non-conceptual presence of being and activating that space that's appreciating. To Be!

We are faced with many obstacles, be it sadness, anger or hurt which then affects the balance of happy and sad brain chemicals called neurotransmitters. When sad and low, the isolating darkness may be seen as "My mind is like a bad neighbourhood, I don't like going there alone!" "My stomach is in a knot" attests to moods changes connecting the gut to the brain.

Change the neurochemistry with mindful awareness! As the body, mind and spirit come into alignment, the happy brain chemicals can be ignited and women will be inspired!

Vanita Dahia is an Integrative Medicine Pharmacist from Melbourne, Australia

Inspiration 040

A Goddess's Encounter with Love

Luisa Russo

To assist her with life's endings, in the energy of the glorious full moon, peace formed tears in her eyes. As she gasped at the realization that goodbye and endings abstractly gifted her with peace. A profound insight, especially as she shares golden threads of light in the bigger wider scheme of things.

Knowing her infinite connection and knowing nothing is ever really disconnected. As she sat in this protective healing light and recieved the peace from this wisdom which her soul longed for. How she would combat this wretched saddness that tore her apart, suddenly became clear in recognising that she was here to experience life and learn soul lessons.

The Goddess called upon her brave as she allowed what she learnt about endings to rise up in her. Soon something magical was shown to her. It was a glowing circle pulsating in time with her heart. It floated above her crown and slowly moved down her body. Embraced in this ring she could feel the gentle vibration moving inside her. Limb to limb. Muscle to muscle. Cells to cells. Breath after breath. And these are the words communicated to her: "I choose to remember the smile, the love in people's eyes as in the end of this physical life, that is all there is ... I am love and I am everywhere and know just where I need to be. If I seem in your face. In your space. I don't mean to be. I know and am not afraid of your fear. I am love and call to your love vibration. I love you."

Luisa Russo is a Spiritual Intuitive from Melbourne, Australia

Inspiration 041

I'm Loving ...

List the things that you most love about reading the inspirational stories in the Book of Inspiration.

Inspiration 042

Crossroads

Tanya Chambers

Meet Me at the Crossroads
My Darling Friend...
Two Broken Hearts
We Have to MEND...

OUR Souls feel Buried
Beneath the EARTH...
Meet ME at the CROSSROADS
To Experience Rebirth...

NORTH... !!! SOUTH... !!!
EAST... !!! WEST... !!!
4 Routes to Choose...
Which 1 is BEST...?

So Hurry Along
Make NO Mistake...
Meet ME at the CROSSROADS
WE have Decisions to Make...

DIVINE Intervention
May Play a ROLE...
But Between US
WE only have 1 GOAL...

To FIND the Happiness
WE Both Deserve...
Meet ME at the CROSSROADS
OUR Seats are Reserved...

The TRAIN sets OFF
WE are BOTH on Board...
There's a WORLD out there
To be Explored...

This Train runs Smoothly
Along Its Track...
MEET ME at the CROSSROADS
There's NO Going Back...

By Tanya
For Tanya
Love Tanya

Tanya Chambers

Inspiration 043

Career Choices

Cille Harris

Math and science came naturally to me, all through school. In 1974, when it came time to decide on university, I was stumped. A visit to the guidance office surprised me when I heard, "You should be an engineer." I didn't even know what an engineer was! Where is she now, this woman who opened up a whole new world for me? How can I thank her from the bottom of my heart? Perhaps, by sharing my story I will honour her and inspire you to discover and embrace your skills and talents, to follow your passions.

I graduated from engineering, married my dear husband, enjoyed a successful job, birthed four amazing sons, earned a Masters degree in Business and launched my own consulting business as a professional facilitator. Besides all the transformational client projects that I completed, my most memorable moments were created doing volunteer and pro-bono work for my profession and my community.

I could not have predicted this path. Just follow your passions and your life will take you on an amazing journey.

Cille Harris is a Facilitator
from Ompah, Canada

Inspiration 044

Just Get Started

Jessica Savic

Fear always evoked feelings of helplessness in me, so I began to ask myself: "How would I behave if I couldn't get the task or challenge at hand wrong? If I wasn't afraid of looking stupid, or feeling insignificant?"

You don't need to be great to get started, but you do need to get started to be great.

You shouldn't judge yourself based on how many times you've failed, but instead on how fast you get up, dust yourself off and keep moving.

What I have learnt as a certainty is that moment you feel fear arising, and decide to tackle the challenge anyway, the deepest struggle you are experiencing will allow you to produce your greatest successes, and in turn, will instill within you your greatest strengths.

So I urge you to take a deep breath and keep moving. Always remember that you're worth it!

Jessica Savic is an Online Marketing Coach from Melbourne, Australia

Strive for Contentment

Tracey Maclay

I've come to realise that 'happiness' is just an illusion. A more easily attainable goal is to strive for 'contentment' in life. We wouldn't have a the full spectrum of feelings available to us if we were meant to be continually happy! (Patanjali yoga sutras.) Remember you are not in charge of anyone but yourself and you are not responsible for anyone else's happiness. So get out there and do something that is meaningful to you. Yoga philosophy teaches that what you give out in positive energy comes back to you in this life and hopefully the next.

Meditation teaches us how to observe our thoughts before we respond and to remember to do this in daily life. This takes practice and concentration. Meditation helps to calm your 'monkey mind' from jumping around from one thought to another. Character is made up of repeated habits. We can choose to change our habits. Make it a habit to meditate at least twice a week and then progress to daily. Start with two minutes and five breaths without any other thought creeping in. If you falter, start again. Prana is your energy force which is awakened using your breathing techniques. Feel the movement of your breath from your lower stomach right up to your throat and back down again.

Tracey Maclay is an Early Childhood Teacher and Yoga Teacher from Brisbane, Queensland

Inspiration 046

You Can Only Control You

Robyn Nelson

What other people do is out of your control. What other people say is out of your control. How people react to anything you do or say is out of your control! Literally the only person you can control is you. What you say, what you do … Your reactions and responses … They are the things you have 100% control over.

If there are areas in your life where you are frustrated and annoyed, chances are you are trying to control other people in some way. This won't lead to a happy life.

You can offer advice, give direction, have conversations and counsel… You can do many things to help people reach a common ground of understanding, but that doesn't mean you can in any way control what other people do.

When you reach a place where you accept people exactly as they are, you will find peace. A place where you are no longer controlled by the external world. Instead, you'll be more able to use your inbuilt self-control in all areas of your life.

This will bring you peace.

*Robyn Nelson is an Entrepreneurial Mentor
from Brisbane, Queensland*

Inspiration 047

The Butterfly Effect

Jo Schutt

In my comparatively short amount of years in business I've gone through an incredibly large amount of change and transition. However, from a very young age I've wanted to be the one to make change, to take action and follow my passions. My business journey has certainly been one that reflects this philosophy.

The first attempt was butterfly wall hangings in the garage when my children were tiny, which lead to creating a natural therapy resource for conception, pregnancy and parenting to then running a major annual event and creating a networking group for women in business, which lead to opening a venue with a commercial lease in partnership with my business soul-mate.

Every change I've made or new venture I've embarked on has been inspired or sparked by a conversation, a gut feeling, an impulse to make change and 'be the change'. And while I encourage anyone starting out in business to have a well thought out plan, do the market research and find out how viable your business has the potential to be, I also strongly encourage you to go with the flow, follow your passion and listen to your intuition – it will tell you more than the figures on a cash flow forecast!

Jo Schutt is a Business Mentor and Growth Facilitator from Melbourne, Australia

Inspiration 048

Be Inspired

Blaise van Hecke

Often we wait for the right conditions for our life to be perfect, and then we'll feel happy and successful. But if we wait for the perfect conditions our life might pass by and we will be full of regrets.

Think about it. If we waited until we could afford to have children, we will miss having them when we are young enough to enjoy them. Let's face it, can we ever 'afford' to have children? Life isn't something that can be planned to the nth degree. Things happen that are out of our control. Health and job security can only be controlled to a point.

So live life with passion. Be inspired by opportunities that surround you every day. Don't wait. Don't wait for inspiration to hit because it may never come. Life is part inspiration, part perspiration, so go out there and make it happen. Say yes to life!

Blaise van Hecke is an award-winning Writer and Publisher from Melbourne, Australia

Inspiration 049

Baby Steps

Gaya Pedris

Hues of Calm and Soft Lullabies
Gurgling Slurps and Little Cries
Oh Little One please don't weep
Gently and Tenderly we'll rock you to sleep
Mummy and Daddy will watch you close
As you dream your dreams
And softly doze

We long to hold you in our arms
And keep you safe from all life's harms
But first we need to learn to walk
Baby Steps before we talk

So Slowly, slowly we have learned
To walk these steps that we have earned

And step by step we do our part
Our thoughts are filled with our Little Lark
The only alarms to be heard
Will be the heartbeats a flutter
of our little herd

When a warm tight hug
Will be our only drug
Cuddles and Giggles our only dose
Watching the pitter patter
Of your little toes

We'll laugh, we'll weep
We'll scream with joy
For our little Girl and our little Boy
Taught us well
that in our Life

Baby Steps we have to take

For all Our Dreams
A reality to Make!

Gaya Pedris is a Mum and Laundrette Owner
from Melbourne, Australia

Inspiration 050

Miracles 3

Gaya Pedris

The road we started on was Narrow and Broken
It was hard for these words to even be spoken
But suddenly, it dawned on me
That Miracles may come in Three

Really? Truly? Could this be?

Should I be scared?
Was something wrong?
I know we had to learn to crawl
But now we walk; We talk;

We even run
Everyone is having
So much fun

One more soon
To join our Brood
The more, the merrier
for the mood!

And just like that we were told
Yes, another healthy heart
to Have and Hold

This time Lord you Blessed us all
You chose me to carry
our Miracles small
You've chosen us
with no fuss
No Worry, no Fear
Not a single Tear

Our new Miracle will grow and grow
She'll fill our lives with love
and that warm infectious Glow

Our Little Angel
This you knew
Through you
God Blessed the Broken Road
that led us straight to YOU!

Gaya Pedris is a Mum and Laundrette Owner
from Melbourne, Australia

Inspiration 051

A Wise Woman

Andrea Rodriguez

A wise woman shared with me, "When confronted with a mountain (problem/challenge) you have two choices – you can either try and go up the mountain and struggle, get tired, defeated, and consequently fall back or it might take longer but by going around the mountain you actually overcome (problem/challenge) and win the victory." This wise woman was my mother who always gave me wisdom and supported me in my difficult times.

This is just one of many pearls of wisdom that Mum shared with me, and it has certainly helped me through many challenges including overcoming breast cancer, losing my mum, divorce, and sometimes just everyday life. Life can be full of challenges but what I have learnt and found is that we have the strength within to be empowered and always moving forward.

No matter how hard life can get, always look at the brighter side of life.

There will always be someone who is willing to help and guide you or just a shoulder to cry on.

Andrea Rodriguez is a Disability Support Worker from Melbourne, Australia

Inspiration 052

Are You Being Selfish?

Trish Springsteen

"Sometimes all you need is just 20 seconds of insane courage. Just literally 20 seconds of embarrassing bravery and I promise you something great will come from it."
– Benjamin Mee, *We Bought a Zoo*

I often hear the words, "No I can't get up to speak, speaking makes me nervous, I don't want to be a professional speaker." My answer is don't be selfish! Sounds harsh perhaps, however, just think: one word, one sentence, one phrase that you share in your message could be just what a person in your audience needs to hear to make a profound change in their life. By not sharing your message you could be depriving that person of that change. Can you really be that selfish that you would let your nerves, your fear, your inaction stop you from sharing your message?

So take 20 seconds of insane bravery, breathe and step up and share your passion, your message with those who need to hear it. Just 20 seconds to start speaking, 20 seconds to pick up the phone, 20 seconds to stand up at a network meeting and amazing things will happen.

Don't be selfish – it's not about you – it's always about them.

Trish Springsteen is a Speaker, Mentor, Coach, Author and Radio Host from Brisbane, Queensland

Inspiration 053

Something Good for Someone Else

Julie White

We've all been there, those days and times in life where we really just feel we can't take on the world, in any way, shape or form. The thing is, though, while we are in this place, although we may not think so at the time, it is no different to any other day in the fact that we still have choices. In the words of Johnette Napolitano, "It's time to crash and burn or fly." None of us want to crash and burn, so how do we fly?

Something that has always got me by is my belief that when things aren't going your way, or you are feeling bad about yourself, go and do something good for someone else. The old adage, that there is always someone worse off than you, rings so true. So go take your mind off yourself and see how you can light up the life of another and in doing so find your own light and happiness.

Julie White is an Author and an Education Governance from Melbourne, Australia

Inspiration 054

AHA! AHA! Moment in Collaboration

Carol-Chantal Séguin

When I founded WOW in Montreal, back in 2012, I didn't think the networking group would expand with such fervor. You see, I moved back home in Ottawa, in 2015, to be the primary caregiver to my mother who was recovering from brain surgery and a subsequent stroke. The only thing giving me a break from the daily routine were WOW Ambassador activities. They kept me in a positive mood and inspired me to continue with the motto/vision/growth of the "Women helping Women" community. Always driven to help others achieve business success, my philosophy is together we can accomplish so much more, by learning, supporting and encouraging one another.

My "Aha! Aha!" moment came at a vendor show where I suggested to competitors that they should combine their tables to make one bigger, more attractive display. WE need to learn to "play in the same sandbox". Their booth had the most client engagement that day! I love motivating, inspiring and mentoring entrepreneurs. Every day I am blessed to be surrounded by amazing women! As much as I hope to inspire these women, they have likewise inspired me.

*Carol-Chantal Séguin is a Business Coach
from Ottawa, Canada*

Inspiration 055

Legacy Of An Abundant Life...

Yolanda Alvares

Not one of us is exempt from the legacy of living an abundant life and the only thing that can keep us from this legacy is our belief that we do not deserve such a legacy.

Here are 3 steps by which you can choose to claim your rightful legacy for an abundant life:

1. Self-love: unless we take the time to nurture ourselves daily, i.e. fill our own cup, can we truly give of ourselves wholly to those who matter to us. We must fill our cup so that we can truly give from an overflowing cup.
2. Trust: Trust that there are no coincidences and that everything is on purpose. When faced with challenges, trust that you are 'perfect' exactly the way you are to face this challenge. Trusting that the lessons that you will learn from this challenge are exactly what you need to grow into the person you were always meant to become.
3. I am Enough: Know that you are enough just as you are. There is nothing more you need to be, do or have. You are enough. Repeat the words 'I am enough' several times each day, and you will begin to feel a sense of being truly abundant.

Yolanda Alvares is an Empowerment Coach from Melbourne, Australia

Truth

Adrienne Gaha-Morris

I started my life in Sydney, NSW, then moved to Newcastle for my mother's job when I was eight. I was a very bright girl being in a Gifted and Talented class for year 5 and 6 and then I started at a selective high school.

My whole life changed when I was diagnosed with an inoperable Arteriovenous Malformation in my brain when I was 12. I spent the best part of the next eight years in hospital and I was knocking on death's door quite a few times.

My mother was my strength when I needed it and she always stayed with me in the hospital and supported me through my recoveries. I came out the other side and I now feel a drive to affect other lives in a profound way.

Now I have a different view on life. I am not scared of death, as I used to be, having sleeping problems as young as three because I didn't want to die in my sleep. I have a profound trust in my reason for being on this earth and I have a difference to make before I leave.

Adrienne Gaha-Morris is Self-Employed from Brisbane, Australia

Inspiration 057

Cycles of Life

Roz Tilley

Life progresses, not always as we wish. Take heart and dig deep, you are only given what you can handle and for some I can hear you ask "How would you know?" I know because I have lived it. My gauge was one good day in seventeen and I realised I was going to succeed when that number reversed itself to one bad day in seventeen. I didn't look too far in either direction and I would tell you as others told me "just be in the now" the most frustrating statement when all I wanted to do was to dig myself deeper into self pity and self destruction. I found my inner strength and like me it is available for you too.

Work on changing the internal dialogue, it will keep you on track. Be constant with yourself and take baby steps to a stronger you. No longer will playing the victim support you anymore. If you can own the strength to your part of what has happened to you, your healing will begin in earnest. You can do it, I know it. I trust you, can you trust you?

Roz Tilley is an International Teacher, Healer and Author and lives in Warburton, Australia.

Becoming Change

Hannah Nicholson

"I can be changed by what happens to me. But I refuse to be reduced by it."
– Maya Angelou

Change is inevitable in life and the only constant is change. By learning to use this principle, women can harness their power to transform their own lives and the wider community. We need to accept our own experiences to learn and evolve from them, ensuring we grow as individuals. Nothing is ever a mistake but rather a lesson. Continue to grow, learn and nurture yourself to keep evolving. Self-development is the greatest tool we have at our disposal. When we change ourselves we can assist others in their journey. We are all one; help others as they you. Use your own power to bring goodness into the world.

Do not be afraid of what is within you, power and courage come from within. Never stop yearning for knowledge and wisdom, as your experiences encompass your being.

We determine our own happiness. Life is complex but it is a subjective experience and you are in charge of your own future. You always have a choice; choose wisely.

Hannah Nicholson is a Student from Melbourne, Australia

Inspiration 059

You Are Perfect

Jose Toussaint

I grew up with a very, "I can do" attitude. Growing up and raised by my dad as a primary carer, because of my mother being an invalid, made me different from most kids in my day. I didn't relate to female energy very well. I started to make friendships with women in my mid thirties because I became a mother to a beautiful girl, in a foreign country and a foreign town.

Giving birth to a child was a real shock! I had to take my barriers down. That was the scariest thing ever! I learnt from other women how to be a mother and much self-healing was done. I have learnt and seen anything in life is possible and I do feel truly blessed that I am able to support other women in their journey of going where they want.

Women need to celebrate their cycles of life, to understand there is wisdom behind every season. I am grateful for these women who have helped me on my journey of celebrating being a woman. I can pass this on to my daughter and hopefully she will pass it on too.

Jose Toussaint is a Kinesiologist, Hypnotherapist and Coach from Brisbane, Australia

Inspiration 060

Self-Belief

Georgia Varjas

Today, I believe in myself. I know I am unique. I have my own smile, laugh and hair! I have my own distinctive voice and my individual thoughts, my generous heart and my experiences that have created my unique style of words. Today, I have the confidence to embrace all my "differences" and see them as positive attributes. It has taken me a few years to understand and clean up the negative talk I heard and digested during my childhood and beyond.

Do you remember that negative talk? "That's bad, that's dirty, don't do that … You'll never be good at anything. Cross your legs … Open your legs, that's bad, that's dirty."

Being a rebel is a tricky and sometimes slippery road … but for me, it was the only way out of all that conditioning and negative blurb. It put the lines on my face and creases on my fingertips and made me into the vital person I am today. It took a spoonful or two of courage – to accept and love my 'out of the comfort zone' way of living.

Every time I started a new business venture, I always made myself the first client, the first customer, and gave myself VIP treatment. Now, today, I believe in myself.

Georgia Varjas is a Speaker, Coach and Writer from San Javier, Spain

Inspiration 061

Dear Mum – Thank You

Lani Sharp

"One of the luckiest things in life that can happen to you is, I think, to have happy childhood."
– Agatha Christie

I think one of the best gifts you can ever give your parents is to tell them you had a happy childhood. So this is dedicated to my mother, who is still with us:

Dear Mum, thank you for my happy childhood. You gave me the love to flourish, the courage to be my true self, the encouragement to allow my passions to unfold, the confidence for my natural talents to shine through, and the wings to fly into the realms of deep imagination. You blessed me with the gift of freedom to be myself, and the space to have long periods of solitude during which I wrote things that would hopefully one day become literary masterpieces. Thank you for helping to shape the person I am today – powerful beyond measure, free-spirited, and utterly inspired. Thank you, above all, for not only encouraging me to follow my heart, my bliss, and my dreams, but also for genuinely believing in those dreams throughout my childhood and beyond. All my dreams are coming true today because of you.

Thank you Mum, for my happy childhood.

Lani Sharp is an Author, Astrologer, Healer, Lightworker and Eternal Student of Magic from Melbourne, Australia

Inspiration 062

Sisters...

Ashleigh Andrews

Protect your sisters! If there is anyone a woman should be able to count on, it is another woman. But too often we are the first to judge. We shouldn't view one another's existence as a competition, but an opportunity to love, help, learn, and bond with other women of this world.

Mothers, grandmothers, girlfriends, trans-women, women of colour, sisters, aunts! Build each other up! Society wants us to compare ourselves to other women. They hold us back by making us tear each other down. In school, at work, on the street and in our families. Don't give in!

Imagine how far we could go if we could let go of what we have always been trained to do, comparing every woman with that impossible perfect image. She's too bossy, she's too meek, she has too many kids, she's not thin enough, she doesn't want kids!?

No "kind" of woman is better or worse than any other, no matter her position in life. The level of love and support we open ourselves to by supporting other women is unlike anything else in this world!

Ashleigh Andrews is an Undergrad, aspiring Author and Editor from Melbourne, Australia

Inspiration 063

Today and Tomorrow

Monika Miller

If I could speak to myself as a child or teenager, I would say to her, "I am thankful and so grateful for you. Yes YOU! You are born with a beautiful, radiant and powerful heart. God/Universe makes no mistakes, only treasures. There are times when you will not feel that radiant or powerful. In those times, remember, nothing is broken. It is simply a moment in time when there is something you are learning about yourself and others. This is an important part of the magnificent plan to help you expand, learn and grow."

"You are like a seed preparing to bloom. Nurture, speak kind words and be grateful for you. Guaranteed, things always change. Remember, YOU are powerful! How? You can help grow the change! You always have a choice. No matter what. If something does not feel right, that is your inner guidance speaking to you. Listen to it and allow it to guide you. You are never, ever alone. Breathe, pause and let go of the struggle, with baby steps, until you feel spirit guiding you. It is always there and always has your back."

"Believe in you, with much love."

Monika Miller is a registered Reflexologist and Children's Yoga Teacher from Ottawa, Canada

Inspiration 064

Your HEART Matters

Gill Barham

Have you heard the saying, "Hindsight is a wonderful thing"? If you were with me in November 2012, we are with a petite, grey haired lady, Dawn, who wears glasses and a blue nurse's uniform. "Well Gill, your results aren't great, your weight has rocketed and you seem very low. Tell me, have you had any thoughts of harming yourself?"

What? How wrong could she get it? I have a great family, a nice home, a good job, I juggle everything and everybody nicely. In fact, I am practically superwoman! That's a ridiculous thing to ask me, of all people.

But you see, Dawn saw something that I couldn't. Looking back at the previous three years, in "hindsight", I could see that the "job" was damaging my heart; both the one inside me, and the one I have to give to the world. I was becoming a carbon copy of my mother who died at 56 when I was 28 years old and 30 weeks pregnant with my first daughter. What message was I giving to my daughters, now in their twenties? Was I setting a good example, or, like Mum, a horrible warning?

Can YOU find a better way to "be" in the world, working on "purpose", leaving a legacy? It's important, because Your HEART Matters.

*Gill Barham is a Lifestyle Coach
from Corby, United Kingdom*

Inspiration 065

Never Give Up!

Marie Ferguson

I heard somewhere that "attitude is everything". In many ways I totally agree with that saying, but you can only go so far. Gratitude gives you the solid foundation to build from. You know where you are, you know who can support you, even if it's just yourself.

Find what inspires you and gives you joy. You don't need to tell everyone. You just need something to keep you from giving up or giving in when the world tries to get you down.

You need to find your own vision. Sometimes it is from your experience, from your education or just from something you have seen that seems totally wrong and needs to be righted. And it is you that needs to be the one to do it. Finally, you know that there will be challenges. People will not make it easy for you. It takes time to gain trust, become known and liked. So never give up!

Key things to remember:

- To be part of life you need to do the work of life.
- Maintain your social and emotional skills to feel connected to world.
- Have high expectations of yourself. If you don't meet them straight away, try and try again.

Marie Ferguson is a Financial Planner and Mortgage Broker from Sydney, Australia

Inspiration 066

Moving Forward

Ana-Rosa Avendano

Ever since I can remember, I always wanted to get married, have a white picket fence and a dinner table full of kids, five to be exact. I did get married at 26 and had my first child at 27. Two more beautiful girls followed.

I never knew that the love I have for my girls would be so great, that I would sacrifice everything for them and their wellbeing. For me, my three girls are my inspiration and the drive for me to keep going in good times and bad.

I try to be a super mum – I know I'm not, but deep down inside I know I have tried my best, and to me that's more than enough. Though, half the time I'm extremely tired and I drive around with my eyes half closed. When I look at my beautiful girls – always happy, always laughing – thats all I need to continue doing what I do on a daily basis.

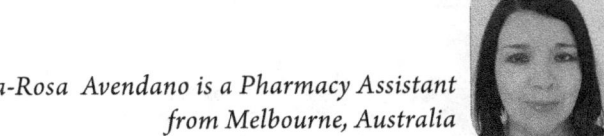

Ana-Rosa Avendano is a Pharmacy Assistant from Melbourne, Australia

Inspiration 067

Follow Your Passion

Marilou Coombe

I have travelled the world; 6 continents; 33 countries and 65 cities! All before I was 30. Some people believe you need loads of money to do this. Many times I was told I could not do it and that I needed to focus on tangible dreams. Not so!

Travel was, and still is, my passion. I did whatever it took to make it happen. This included working in the travel industry for a while, living in different countries so that I could have easier access to travel. I followed my heart and am so excited by the life I have lived and the places I have visited. Not to mention the endless connections I have made and new experiences I had.

I made lists. I set goals. I created vision boards. I got clear on what I wanted and where I wanted to be. The universe always tended to provide … because I wanted it so much I found ways to make it happen.

Dream big! And follow your passion ... this is the only way to live.

My question to you is – What are you passionate about? How are you living your passion each day? And when obstacles arise, how are you overcoming them?

Marilou Coombe is a Coach, Mentor and Trainer from Melbourne, Australia

Ignite Your Light

Nikki Simmos

Two accounts of rape, forced abortion and suicidal thoughts happened and unfortunately at seventeen it happened to me. Life is about Freedom Within Your Soul. To be able to live your life and be the best version of yourself that you possibly can be.

An awareness of faith, love, beliefs, values and strength must come from within you to achieve what you want. Only then can you truly let go and move on.

Nikki Simmos is a Specialist Teacher, Coach, Counselor, Author, Speaker and Mentor from Melbourne, Australia

Inspiration 069

Make Good Choices

Lynda Holt

From the beginning, I knew my life would be different from others as I was born with Spina Bifida. For me even the simplest tasks required thought and planning so that I could learn to become independent.

Surgery after surgery would be required from an early age. That definitely took a toll on my mental and physical health and continued throughout my life. Early on I spent some time in a Children's Home, I was consistently told that I would not amount to anything and that I would presumably spend my life in and out of jail. I knew I was made of better stock and that everyone has the ability to take a path in life, that can lead them to become successful.

Looking back, I can say that I've accomplished a lot. I'd cared for two foster children by the age of 19, won a Silver Medal at the 2000 Sydney Paralympics and now own my own Personal Development company, all from my wheelchair. Success has come from a lot of hard work, perseverance and self-belief.

You may not be able to change what happens to you but you can choose how you'll handle it. What will you choose?

Lynda Holt is Director, NLP Trainer and Clinical Hypnotherapist from Sydney, Australia

Inspiration 070

Letting Go!

Maurissa Ailion

"Holding on is believing that there's only a past, letting go is knowing that there's a future."
– Daphne Rose Kingma

'Letting go' when something or someone prevents you from living your life to the fullest is one of life's toughest lessons; I too have found this very challenging in matters of the heart, family relationships and work. Especially when feeling stuck or a sense of heaviness prevails that seems unable to be shifted. Whether it's anger, guilt, love, loss or betrayal, change never comes easy. We struggle to hold on and we struggle to let go.

It is only by letting go that we are able to move on with our lives. It is only by letting go that we can forgive and hopefully integrate the situation as part of our herstory and perhaps begin to forget. Letting go doesn't mean that we don't care about someone or something anymore. It just means that you come to realise that the only thing you truly have control over is yourself.

In matters of the heart, deep down within ourselves we sense when it's time let go and time to create a new chapter in our life. We often know this intuitively and perhaps from things said by those closest to us or we have sought counselling to sort out these blocked threads in our life.

*Maurissa Ailion is a Counsellor
from Adelaide, Australia*

Inspiration 071

Growing in Kindness and Love

Joahnne Sperling

I am a little girl with a dream. I love all girls in the world, you are all beautiful and precious to me, I see you all as my sisters in God. I wish I can find a way to let you know we can learn from our mistakes to grow stronger and we are not too small to show adults how to feel loved and what kindness means.

I wish you to know that you can stand up against bullying and never let other children put you down. If that happens, just walk away and forgive because they are already below you when they are hurting you. Keep your head up and smile. I wish you to show gratefulness to people, even when someone brings you a gift you don't really like – smile and say thank you.

Never give up on your dreams because of other people's opinions – always follow your heart. You know, I can give you my hand to come to my home to play with my toys just to make you happy, I can share my clothes and food with you too. I can teach you to sing a happy song and dance with me, and if you are blind I can guide you anywhere to protect you…but your happiness is already inside you, it doesn't come from the outside world.

I wish you can know that believing in God will always make you feel loved and so you know that you are a girl capable to achieve what you want. Love yourself – Be yourself growing in kindness and love.

Joahnne Sperling is a Student
(sometimes a Fairy, sometimes a butterfly)
from Sydney, Australia

Inspiration 072

Girls, We Got This!

Josie Kearsey

I have met women from all walks of life and one message rings true, the attitude and meaning we apply to life reflects the texture and fabric of our soul. Our tenacity and resolve are the cornerstones we build our strength and courage to say, "I GOT THIS."

While life is easy to some, to others it takes a little more self talk and convincing that, "YOU GOT THIS." Should harsh disappointments and hurts make you cry like a baby, remember, "YOU GOT THIS." If you see the glass half empty, stand on your head and see it is actually half full, because, "YOU GOT THIS." If you cry a trillion tears for lost opportunities, irretrievable words, actions or the agony of losing someone, take a deep breath, because, "YOU GOT THIS."

If the School of Life stops you, don't be robbed, look on the flip side, own the triumphs, achievements and accomplishments, savour them, they are your victorious trophies, because, "YOU GOT THS!" If the voice of self doubt screams into your ears and echoes into your soul, shout back louder, "I GOT THIS." If answers are slow to arrive, keep singing this lullaby, "I GOT THIS." If grandiose plans go to mud and you can't seem to start again, whisper, "I GOT THIS." How do I know all this? Simple, I live by these three little words and they make all the difference.

I GOT THIS! Have you?

*Josie Kearsey is an Event Director
from Melbourne, Australia*

Inspiration 073

Proud to Be a Woman

Sonja Koukounaras

Y ou are Beautiful.

You are Compassionate ~ You are Strong ~ You are Confident ~ You are Fierce ~ You are Forgiving ~ You are Loving ~ You are Determined~ You are Worthy ~ You are Imperfect ~ You have to believe in yourself when no one else does.

Be unstoppable despite your doubts, despite your failures, push on because of them.

Don't listen to the people who say you cannot handle what the storm will bring ... BE THE STORM!

When Women support other Women ... amazing things happen.

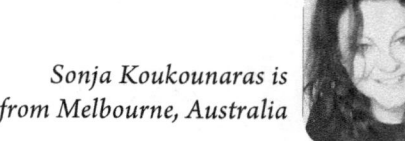

Sonja Koukounaras is from Melbourne, Australia

Inspiration 074

Connection to Self

Shani Suttie

After years of struggling with control and abuse in my life, I realised that I am the CREATOR. Instead of looking at the challenging stuff as unwanted experiences, I began to embrace them as opportunities for healing, growing and learning. I realised that I was responsible for my own experiences. From there I could transcend and become the GREATER SELF that I AM.

The MOST IMPORTANT thing for me: CONNECTION TO SELF.

I was running most of my life looking for things on the outside to fill up the emptiness inside of me, trying to validate myself and feel lovable. The disconnection became greater, the more I ran my life on a negative playing field, which then attracted more negativity into my life. The outside was a reflection of what was going on for ME on the inside.

I began to let go of control, I moved into my heart space and creating from this point became fun, joyous and flowed with synchronicity and miracles. I awakened to my truth: I AM LOVE. From there, I have been creating from a beautiful place, which in turn has brought so much beauty, joy and abundance into my life. Breathwork helped me connect easily and gently.

Self Connection ~ Healing ~ Empowerment ~ Creating = LOVE

Shani Suttie is a Breathwork Facilitator from Brisbane, Queensland

Inspiration 075

Suddenly Homeless

Annie Toscher

Growing up on the south coast beaches of NSW's Australia seemed like an idyllic childhood. To the outside world our family life looked wonderful. Behind closed doors life was volatile with fighting parents that instilled fear into my little body. It all came crashing down when my father beat my mother so badly she left.

My sisters and I moved to Newcastle with my father. In a short time my sisters returned to Wollongong and lived with my mother. I was not wanted by either of my parents as they had created a new life and I simply did not belong. I felt unlovable and fearful for my safety and my stepmother's father was molesting me.

My world came crashing down at 17 when my father punched me in the face and knocked out my front tooth. Suddenly I became homeless. That event was my transformational turning point when I chose not to be a victim. I embarked on a path of personal and spiritual development, empowering transformational change for others.

Annie Toscher is a Matrix Therapist, Passion and Purpose Coach, and Co-Author of "You Can Be Your Own Stylists" from Melbourne, Australia

Inspiration 076

Attitude is Everything

Elaine Squiers

Many defining experiences in my 70 years have changed and impacted my life. None more so than, when unemployed, I was offered a "business opportunity" for $22,000 (all I had) by a shonky businessman. I later discovered the opportunity he promised was not achievable. Result: he levelled me financially, forcing me to sell my home. Living on Centrelink income only, no home, no savings left, I had to think quickly outside the box. It was quite challenging learning to be resilient, survive on little income, willing to work at any low paid job offered. Even travelling north to Newman in W.A. cleaning cars on a mine site, which I found challenging and exciting.

Returning to Perth, I applied to my previous employer and was successfully re-employed again and still work there to this day. Thank God for my health and energy. In 2015 I became a published author. My book is called *A Healthy Lifestyle in Your Golden Years* and through coaching I assist people to live a healthier life. Learning about oils and essences, organic farming and growing my own vegetables and fruit adding to my armoury. Nick Vujicic's book *Life Without Limits* really inspired me to just find my life's purpose, a way to do it, and work hard to achieve it. My age is no barrier. How inspiring is that?

Elaine Squiers is an Author and Health Coach,
Qualified by Experience from Perth, Australia

Inspiration 077

In my Youth, I Wish That:

Carlyn Ryklief

In my youth, I wish that: I knew that my worth is not relative, that other people's opinions of me is a reflection of them first. I had explored the magic, mystery and wonder of life instead of my fears. I had discovered this quote:

This is the true joy in life, the being used for a purpose recognized by yourself as a mighty one; the being a force of nature instead of a feverish, selfish little clod of ailments and grievances complaining that the world will not devote itself to making you happy.

I am of the opinion that my life belongs to the whole community, and as long as I live it is my privilege to do for it whatever I can.

I want to be thoroughly used up when I die, for the harder I work, the more I live. I rejoice in life for its own sake. Life is no "brief candle" for me. It is a sort of splendid torch which I have got hold of for the moment, and I want to make it burn as brightly as possible before handing it on to future generations.

– George Bernard Shaw

Carlyn Ryklief is a Teacher from Gisborne, New Zealand

Inspiration 078

Focus on the Positives

Kaz Lock Clarke

My life was turned on its head in 2015. Through various events I lost my life and everything I stood for in April that year. Family stood by my bedside willing me to live, their hearts breaking as I was slipping away. With their love and the expert help of some amazing Critical Care staff, I managed to defy the odds and survive, getting stronger week after week, after week.

I had been dealt a blow unlike any I had ever experienced, PTSD, depression, blood clots, hernias and I was now an Ostomate!

Through this I realised I must have been given a purpose for surviving (I'm a huge believer in things happening for a reason), but what was the reason? My journey was to find the reason – and I did!

My life was a gift, my love was unconditional, my family meant the world and I realised I had abounding knowledge to offer. See, we sometimes need a bad thing to happen to promote the best in us all. Don't see the negative, focus on the positive.

Kaz Lock Clarke is an Ostomate and Support Group Founder from Bendigo Australia

Inspiration 079

'I wouldn't miss this for the World'

Eleisha McInnes

I am a realist, I live for the now with a rather substantial nod to my past. I don't look into a crystal ball to see my future because what will be, will be.

Growing up we spent a lot of time camping out west, visited Coochie Mudlo Island where we hired rusty old bikes, caught the water taxi to Stradbroke Island where we bussed and walked around the island. I also enjoyed bushwalking, ice-skating and gymnastics.

When I was 16, Mum remarried and had my little bro. Shortly after I was diagnosed with a brain disorder, we travelled the world to find treatment to no avail. I am now in a wheelchair, I have had to adjust my expectations of life, but I am making the most of it ... Life is beautiful. I am also fed through a tube and I cannot speak. My preferred method of communication is sign language, it is more fluid and my full time carer is very proficient at understanding me ... we have fun conversations, I can honestly say I feel joy when I sign. I have a lightwriter (like a talking typewriter). I am not the fastest typist, seeing as I type with my right hand only, communication this way is slow. But looking at my situation positively (which is a habit of mine), I realise how very lucky I am to be living in this technological era.

In the words of one of my heroes, Garth Brooks: 'I wouldn't miss this for the world.'

Eleisha McInnes is a Realist from Kin Kin Queensland, Australia

Inspiration 080

Forgive – Your Way to Success

Ruth Cyster-Stuettgen

Is this something you can freely say when you are in the depths of despair and see no end to unhappiness? "I'm sorry, please forgive me, thank you, I love you." Unhappiness you think someone you once loved to no end, could very well have caused?

I dare to challenge you on this. Yes you can, and yes you will be able to say these words. Words gifted to the world as h'oponopono, the ancient Hawaiian ritual. Seeking forgiveness from others and yes, even ourselves, is the way to moving forward. Key to walking away. Key to turning our backs on adversity. Key to using the lessons learned and turning them into success.

I promise you, when you learn how to master this beautiful and loving art of forgiveness, you will feel lighter, breathe more freely. You will be opening yourself up to the magic of your unique self and your innate greatness. Success will be no option, but await you with open arms.

"I'm sorry, please forgive me, thank you, I love you." This is your gracious way to success.

The magic lies in your heart …

Ruth Cyster-Stuettgen is an Author, Speaker and Coach from Melbourne, Australia

Inspiration 081

Never Quit on a Bad Day

Dhea Bartlett

From the very first day I started my teaching career, I knew I wanted to do something else. Fast forward 8 years, 3 kids, 3 house moves and building and selling a new home, and we were back in Melbourne. I found myself at a jewellery party one Tuesday morning and saw women having fun and buying jewellery. I thought to myself, I can do this ... That was my introduction to direct sales.

I LOVE everything direct selling offers my family. I can earn teaching money without the teaching hours. So why did I succeed when others failed? Because I never quit on a bad day. Yes I had them: cancellation of parties, no shows, massive promises from team members.

I would always turn to my mentor and debrief. I was able to reframe most of my negative thinking before I internalised it and blamed myself. I was coachable and learned from so many mentors. I would read as much as I could and continually revised what I was doing. Why was I able to do all this? My strong why: I didn't buy other peoples issues. So if you are contemplating a career in direct sales be committed, really commited. Be coachable and never quit on a bad day.

Dhea Bartlett is a Networking Professional from Melbourne, Australia

Inspiration 082

Make "You" your Number One Priority

Sue Ritchie

It is really important that you stop putting everyone else's needs before yours. Why? Because when you prioritise taking care of your own health and needs first, then you will show up as the best version of yourself. And your husband, partner, children, family and friends will be the better for it.

The biggest thing that enabled me to move out from being totally stuck in a business that I didn't want to be in, feeling helpless, overweight and unhealthy, was making a decision based on what I wanted for myself. I had to let go of what anybody else might think. As a result I was able to change my life to one of enjoyment, feeling fulfilled and good about myself.

When you love yourself and look after your own needs first, EVERYTHING in your life benefits. You'll be more productive in your work, more energised and healthy, your romantic relationships will flourish and you will be happier, calmer and more fulfilled.

You have to learn to say "no" to things that don't feel right for you. Give yourself time to get really quiet and listen to your body and your inner guidance. You have all the answers you need inside you.

*Sue Ritchie is Your Esctatic Health Mentor
from Derby, United Kingdom*

Inspiration 083

Gratitude:

The three things I am most grateful for today.

Inspiration 084

Be Your Biggest Accomplishment

Sara J Crawford

"Once you learn to appreciate the small things already in your life and to carefully observe the world around you, you will view the world through a whole different lens!"
– Sara J Crawford

Life should be exactly what you envision, so never settle for less! When life throws you a curve ball, there's a reason for it, so follow the curve! Sometimes those curves can take you on the greatest journey life has to offer and some of the greatest things in life come to those who wait patiently! If you are patient and persistent about what you want, and you work hard enough, you can absolutely obtain ANYTHING!

One of the smartest people I've ever met once told me, "People's opinions, are simply obstructions." That just means, you take in and absorb what is valuable to you and YOUR vision in life and disregard the rest. People are always going to have their opinions, but that doesn't make it valid or relevant to you or your ultimate goals! Be the you that you DREAM about, dig deep inside yourself and find what truly makes YOU happy, and shoot for the stars, because even if you land on the moon, you're halfway there!

Sara J Crawford is a Business Owner, Entrepreneur and Radio Host from Ontario, Canada.

God had a Plan for my Life

Ethelwynne Petersen

God's hand in all that He enabled me to do, despite 10 major surgical operations, has been and continues to be revealed to me throughout my life. His grace uplifted me and made me stronger and more aware of His bountiful blessings and love.

I remember my excitement as a precocious four-year old, staying behind with my childless godparents in Kimberley, the diamond city of South Africa. Family strife caused my father to fetch me four years later. My journey led me to giving my heart to Jesus at a gospel gathering at age eight. My life work came with the Girls' Brigade, a major part of my life. God's plan for my life caused me to lose my third born who would have been an invalid. Losing my husband after 27 years of marriage led me to being a leader in my community. God had a plan for my life and that was all that I ever needed to know.

Ethelwynne Petersen is Retired from Cape Town, South Africa

Inspiration 086

Honour Yourself – the Power of Now

Carla Trigo

The Goddess in you, refers to the gift you give yourself when you take action in releasing who you are not, to be more of who you ARE. Working on yourself to better serve you and discover your truth, your treasures, and jewels of life that have been gifted to you. To tap into your knowledge and awaken your wisdom that resides within you. To honour yourself and those around you.

It is when you find yourself stuck in yesterday, trapped in an emotion or a vision that no longer supports you, and you take care of it by releasing it, interrupting it, raising your awareness to change those patterns that keep you in yesterday, and breathe in today where you have all your power, all your focus, and divine assistance to support and guide you.

Self-love is our fuel; it's the foundation for who we are. Everything builds on top of this foundation, and if it isn't solid, life feels shaky. For those of us who have experienced the power of self-love, we can agree that the effects can often feel quite magical. Life begins to move forward with more ease and things begin to magically fall into place. Relationships improve. Health improves. And life begins to feel good – really good. Ridiculously good.

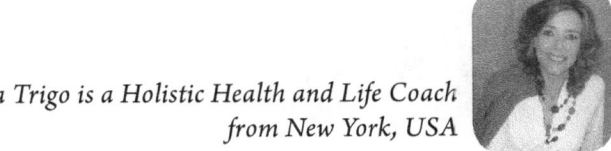

Carla Trigo is a Holistic Health and Life Coach from New York, USA

Inspiration 087

Believe and You Will Achieve

Jenny Scott

I am an everyday person who knows that you can inspire yourself to achieve anything if you put your mind to it. I am aware that a belief is influenced from past experiences, things we've been told and what we've been conditioned to believe. I now know that these beliefs can be changed by the attitude that we choose to take. We need to allow ourselves to believe we can do anything we choose.

The defining moment for me was, after allowing myself to feel intimidated by my brother's achievements, to be told that my older brother believed I had the intelligence and strength to be anything or anyone I wanted to be. The ability to have such power to change our beliefs and thoughts at will is so empowering AND we all have this ability.

If you knew you could handle anything that came your way what would happen?

So: "Feel the fear, face it and just do it."

Jenny Scott is an Artist, Direct Sales Representative from Hastings, Australia

Inspiration 088

Listen to Intuition

Rosemary O'Brien

I'm a professional nurse and have been for over 40 years, so caring for others has been a big part of my life for a long time. The problem is, in caring so much for others, I forgot how to care for myself first. Have you been there? In fact, I've been on a roller coaster of tears, laughter and self-discovery for a long time.

This roller coaster of life takes us on several journeys and we lose ourselves in life and forget the most important person, ourselves, for when we are truly connected to our own inner essence, magic happens within and around us rippling out where ever we go in life.

The short version of my story: I was married for over 20 years, got divorced, lost my soul mate, and raised four sons. I have been bullied, lost everything I owned and… eventually gained the world.

My motto: Listen to your intuition and heart.

Self-love is about taking time to care for yourself, doing things that you enjoy, that make you feel good, allowing your heart to sing and accepting yourself the way you are.

Rosemary O'Brien is a Nurse, and Wellbeing and Life Coach for Professional Women, from Casuarina, Australia

Let Go of the Past

Michal Stewart

All my life I had been bullied, from mild to extreme. Confidence and self-esteem had long vanished. Finally I had the courage to ask myself: Do I want to spend the rest of my life like this? And, more importantly, do I want my past to interfere with my future?

The answers were obvious. I began changing my self-perception. Never easy, but necessary. I read books, joined classes, expanded my horizons. The right people did appear when I needed them and the 'put-me-downs' disappeared. I let go of others' 'stuff'. I let go of my own.

Each day, small steps forward. Some days definitely in reverse. On those days, I allowed myself twenty minutes to rant, rave, sulk, cry. When the time was up, I stopped, dried my eyes, and determined again: this is my life, so I'm in charge.

Now I have an inner confidence. I feel respected. My thoughts and ideas are valued. My wit and sense of humour (both off-beat) have resurfaced. I changed me for me, and am a better person for it. I'm still a 'work in progress' but then, we all are. Give yourself permission to release your past, and enjoy your new you.

Michal Stewart is a Healer from Melbourne, Australia

Inspiration 090

Forge Your Path

Bec Carroll-Bell

Take the path less travelled, or better yet, forge your own. Since I was a little girl I wanted to be a lawyer. It might have been because I liked the lawyer on *A Country Practice*. All through high school I chose subjects and after school activities that would increase my chances of getting in to law at a top tier university.

The day I got my final year 12 results was devastating. I was eight marks short of my goal. Eight marks short of getting into uni. Eight marks short of becoming a lawyer.

I could have accepted a position at a second tier university, but for me, that was not an option. So instead I took a risk and enrolled in a Bachelor of Arts at Wollongong University. I spent my first year of university trying new things, getting good results, and at the end of the year I applied to join the law program. I was accepted. I graduated in 2001 with an Honours Degree in Law.

Be persistent, be creative, find your own path or better yet, forge a new one.

Bec Carroll-Bell is The Everyday Mediator from Melbourne, Australia

Inspiration 091

To the Girl in the Wings ...

Kym Mulcahy

To the girl waiting nervously in the wings, I ask you, 'what if'? What if every woman (including yourself), could truly see how amazing she was? What possibilities would there be?

What if the dreams you had as a little girl were no longer a forgotten fantasy, but a blueprint for something incredible? What if that timid voice (the one you secretly keep inside), was finally given permission to be amplified? You could confidently share your dreams, your vision, and your powerful intuition.

What if instead of playing small and desperately trying to please others, you found the courage to spread your wings and take flight? Imagine what would happen then! What if it was easy to see your unique beauty and talents, and you used them to make a difference? What if you told yourself, 'I'm unstoppable', and knew the world was waiting for you to arrive? And, what if, in your absolute core, you knew you were unequivocally enough? You always have been, and always will be.

I wonder what would happen then? It's time to stop wondering, beautiful. It's time to start believing. You are all this and soooo much more. It's your time to step onto your stage and shine!

Kym Mulcahy is a Personal Branding and Online Business Strategist from Sydney, Australia

Inspiration 092

NOW is the Time!

Kim (Langtip) Wood

Time is short, NOW is the time! You are the designer, the architect of the house (your life) in which you dwell. Think about it for a second … is this the life you truly want?

The most important change we can ever have is a "me-change". Changing our living arrangements, friendship circles, work or relationships doesn't always work long term. We can change the geography as much as we like but until we change the things we carry within us, nothing changes. Letting go of things, forgiveness, gratitude, being true to YOU and willing to grow are the first steps forward. My favourite quotes:

"Don't wait for a light to appear at the end of the tunnel, stride down there and light the bloody thing yourself."
– Sara Henderson

"Be the change you want to see in your world." – Often attributed to Ghandi

The moment I read those, I had the key to my "me-change" and it was up to me, no one else. I pass this key on to you and as you place it into the lock of your future ahead, know that the person writing this believes in you and your change, until you can believe in it yourself. Hugs, Kim.

Kim (Langtip) Wood is a People Builder from Melbourne, Australia

Inspiration 093

I am You, Mum

Emily Jones

I am you, Mum, with drowsy eyes and foggy brain. I've wandered dark halls and rocked in the moonlight. I've wondered if I'm doing this all wrong, am I doing something right, anything? I've smiled and nodded when really I felt lost and lonely, those countless hours wearing me down.

I've landed in this place we call motherhood, a place so much bigger than ourselves. This place where our hearts are walking the earth and fear that I might break them becomes so immobilising that I don't know whether to stay and protect them or run and hide.

I am you, Mum, with your heart so full you nearly burst. I've wandered dark halls and rocked in the sunlight. I've wondered if I'm doing this all right, am I doing something wrong, anything? I've smiled and nodded, I've said I'm having a tough day and been supported, those countless hours shared with others.

I've fallen into this place we call motherhood, something so much bigger than ourselves. This place where our hearts are walking the earth and a pride so immobilising that I don't know whether to stay and watch or run and join in.

I am you, Mum, whatever that may be. You are not alone, this journey is shared and there's a village out there to help. I am you, Mum and there's a safe space here for you.

Emily Jones is a Health and Wellbeing Practitioner, and Entreprenur from Melbourne, Australia

Inspiration 094

Changes

What changes do I choose to make in my life starting today?

Inspiration 095

Seek Happiness

Sara Maynard

For years I suffered with feeling alone. Seems crazy I should say that, as I was always popular with loads of 'friends' around me. The problem I found was the majority of those 'friends' were not actually friends.

One by one those friends would disappear, mainly due to jealousy and envy and also for not accepting me for me, the good and the bad. No matter how much good I did for others it never seemed like enough. I loved and I lost and I would love and lose again. Slowly I felt myself getting lower in mood, my energy decreasing, I no longer felt like ME! My drive and passion for life no longer existed.

It was strangers, who I knew but didn't know, who could see the depression within. I was advised to watch inspiring YouTube videos and read self help books. I also gained advice from others. I finally decided it was time I regained control of MY LIFE! I started to change the way I think and the way I reacted to situations. Slowly but surely things started to get better for me. I set up a private women's group on Facebook called Listen, Uplift, Vent #LUV. I have created a platform for women to be able to listen to each other, uplift each other and also vent to each other without worrying about criticism or judgement.

I am finally in a place where happiness is my main goal! Happy is the new rich!

Sara Maynard is a Dental Administrator from Birmingham, United Kingdom

Inspiration 096

The Art of Self Acceptance

Diana Bonwick

As a woman you are always going to experience the full pallet of emotions. There are no good emotions or bad emotions. There are only more pleasant and less pleasant ones. Don't judge any of them. Hold yourself with deep unconditional love.

Feel the mother of all mothers just below your feet. Be anchored inside your beautiful woman's body and feminine potency. Hold your heart with one hand and your womb with the other.

Acknowledge what is there in that very moment:

… right now I'm feeling sad … resentful … angry … whatever it is … breathe … and just be with what is … fully accepting ALL OF YOU.

Diana Bonwick is a Divine Feminine Business Mentor from Melbourne, Australia

Inspiration 097

Remember

Beth Elaine Haynes

I remember the day you took my innocence
I've been molested she said
I remember the day I found myself alone
I've been abandoned she said
I remember the day you thought you took my womanhood
I've been made to feel shame she said
I remember the day your fist hit my face
I've been assaulted she said
I remember the day I fell to the floor
I've denied she said
I remember the day you left me without food, money or transport
I've had enough she said
I remember the day you walked out the door
I've been set free she said
I remember the day you awakened to me
I've found my voice she said
I remember the day you held out your hand
I've found my connection she said
I remember the day you stood before a crowd and spoke out loud
I've found my freedom you said
I remember the day you looked in the mirror
I've found myself you said   I Remember
I Remember   I Remember you She said .

Beth Elaine Haynes is an Energy Entrepreneur from Brisbane, Australia

Inspiration 098

Seize the Day

Veena Vather

Never give up on your dreams. Like a crusader, fearlessly commit and fight for them. That is after all, your only job in this life, to construct the life you desire. Pursue your dreams with vigor, optimism and enthusiasm because nothing is more appealing or contagious. Do not reconcile yourself with what is, shoot and shoot. If at first you don't hit the mark, keep on keeping on (persevere), my friend, until you hit the mark. Remember Scarlett O' Hara's words in *Gone with the Wind*, "After all … tomorrow is another day." There will be challenges, but you will be pleasantly surprised that if you hold out your hands, seeking help, there will ALWAYS be at least ONE courageous person (if not more!) who will grab them and guide you further along the path of your dreams. Accept the help and take a chance on yourself, back yourself and CHEER yourself on in your life's journey as you would your heroine. There is NO other choice or way to be.

Each day find:

- Someone to love
- Something to smile about
- A tune to dance to
- A song to sing

GOD BE WITH YOU ALWAYS

Veena Vather is a Script Writer from South Africa

Inspiration 099

Give Thanks

Bianca Smith

God will restore my health. I have faced two types of cancer, rheumatoid arthritis, have been well and been too ill. After stopping writing and singing my songs, losing someone very special made me realise life is too short and I cannot simply give up on my dream. Life has never been without challenge but I am here building my empire, living my dream and leaving a legacy for my children. I never thought I would see another day, but not only has God given me the opportunity, but he has me brought me from ashes to soaring in everything I do. This is why I have no other option but to succeed.

My musical journey began through church and family. I always sang, from about age five. My family was very musically talented but I lacked confidence. Now I want the world to hear my voice, to share my gift with the world. Moving from Africa I had to build for my kids, so had to work and support them and my music was on the back burner.

I do what I do for my kids. I give thanks to God that the lymphoma and osteosarcoma are rendered hopeless, and for the strength I have had to push through to find my victory.

Bianca Smith is a Singer/Songwriter from the United Kingdom

Inspiration 100

My World Came Crumbling Down

Maureen Mbondiah Mandipaza

When your world falls apart … *My challenges do not define me* … It wasn't until I learnt to believe in myself that I came to master this affirmation. Growing up in a big family with a complicated background and polygamous affairs meant that I had to learn to survive and above all to believe in myself or I was left to believe in what everyone else perceived of me.

Losing my mother at a tender age of 17 was hard for me and my younger siblings. We had to grow up quickly. So when I found myself in a foreign land in my early 20s with a failed marriage, two children, massive debt, and a repossession order for my property I knew something had to give way. Suddenly the world was crushing down on me. I had no one to answer my questions. Why was I going through this? Where was my lover boy? Where was God in all of this? That's when my journey to self discovery began … I began to search myself … my inner self … what was my purpose?

Maureen Mbondiah Mandipaza is an Entrepreneur Philanthropist from Sedgemoor Park, United Kingdom

Inspiration 101

Unexpected Inspiration

Kathleen Buttigieg

I've always struggled with the word "passion". In fact, growing up the only thing I could ever say I was "passionate" about was how much I hated school. I know others around me enjoyed their experience, but not me. So, as a mother of two boys, I did my greatest acting role ever by choosing to paint a picture of school as being this great experience of fun and learning. Whilst there were some challenging days, overall it was a positive and rewarding time.

It was only through my children that I learnt that school could be fun. It changed my life because through their experiences I was inspired to go back to school. Somewhere along the line, I found my passion – my passion for learning and helping others improve their quality of life. I have been a Health and Wellness Facilitator for over 12 years and I'm still learning skills to add more value.

The life I live today is totally inspired by my children and I would like to honour them and inspire you to make a change in your life that empowers you to live your full potential. You're never too old to learn.

Kathleen Buttigieg is a Reflexoligist/Life Coach from Melbourne, Australia

Inspiration 102

Honour Your Body

Cathy Noël

Your body is the only place where you will get to live for the rest of your life. It is like your best friend, she will always be there for you and will never let you down until your last breath. You love her not because of the way she looks, but for all the good she's bringing in your life. She is perfectly imperfect and this is what makes her so unique and adorable. Don't ever let her compare herself to these unrealistic and unhealthy "beauty standards" made up by Photoshop.

Protect her from any kind of violence. If something bad happens, make sure to give her all the love, time and rest needed for her to recover. Don't let her carry around heavy feelings such as anger, resentment, and guilt. Experience the emotions with her, but never let her hold on to them. Emotions are meant to be lived and released, not to be pushed down and carried. Treat her with your sweetest intentions: feed her with the best nourishment, move and dance with her, give her massages, make her laugh, give her the best quality of sleep but, most of all, celebrate the beauty of life with her.

Cathy Noël is a Speaker, Author and Coach, from Montreal, Canada

Inspiration 103

You Can Do It!

Carol Carson

I was always good at giving positive advice to others, believing in them to take the next step towards their dream. I learned that from my mum. I've been fortunate to have a successful career in the beauty industry, building businesses, travelling the world, enjoying every minute of it.

One day, in a training session, listening to how a company built their prosperous business, a word began to resonate in my head. A word I had heard often and yet it hit me quite suddenly. It was like I was hearing it for the first time, the real meaning of the word to *build*. I knew then that I wanted to build something too. I wanted to build and create my own business. It felt so right because my dad was a builder and now I knew it was my turn to build something for me.

So here I am at the sweet age of 50-ish doing what I've always really wanted to do. I finally gave myself my own advice … believing in myself and knowing I can do it!

"And as we let our own light shine, we unconsciously give other people permission to do the same."
– Marianne Williamson.

Carol Carson is a Business Owner from Derby, England

Inspiration 104

Zak

Leanne Woff

I walked into my six week ultrasound excited to see my third baby for the first time, with my one year-old twins waiting at home. As the doctor put the jelly on my belly, I looked at the monitor next to me in confusion as she said the baby was good. "Only one baby?" I asked, you see I knew what twin scans looked like, I had done this before and although this time round I was convinced I was only having one baby, I could see TWO.

"Well, there are two but it looks like the second one isn't alive, it has no heartbeat," the doctor replied. Devastation. Panic. Disbelief. This could not be happening again. An appointment was made for an emergency scan and as my hubby and I waited we did what we have always done, we prayed, we got our friends to pray. Over the next hour I was extremely sick, making a very big mess at the local Maccas. Finally it was time for the scan. I looked at the screen and again I could see two babies, except this time, the second was TWICE the size he had been. The specialist was confused, he could see TWO perfect little babies, heartbeats and all.

This was Jesus. We prayed and he heard us, as he always does. He did the impossible and my baby doubled in size and grew a heartbeat in ONE HOUR.

Jesus, if you need Him, call Him. He answers. Every time.

Leanne Woff is a Virtual Assistant and Bookkeeper from Melbourne, Australia

Inspiration 105

Friends are Everywhere

Lucy Johnson

If you've gone on a holiday and miss your friends, you should always know that you will see them again. A true friend is always in your heart even when you're apart. It may be days, weeks or even years, but your real friends will always be there for you.

Also, when you're travelling, don't be shy to make new friends. There are little girls and boys around the world who are just as nervous as you, so be brave and ask them to play. No matter what they look like or how they speak they can still be your friend. You never know when you may see them again, in their country, or yours.

Always be kind and open to new friends and look after your old friends well.

Friends are important to share stories with, play games with and have lots of fun with, but they are just as important when you are sad or lonely because they can make you feel better.

Lucy Johnson is an aspiring Circus Performer and Student from Melbourne, Australia

Independent Mom

Cille Harris

"There are only two lasting bequests we can hope to give our children. One of these is roots, the other wings."
– Anonymous

My husband and I are retired engineers, out living the dream. Not long ago, however, one of our four sons was dangerously close to living on the street, after five years of being on his own. We invited him back home to help him figure out what was going on. Gratefully, we were guided by experts to find a diagnosis and a solution. But what about me? How does a Mom let go?

Helping him find his way awakened me to find my independence and freedom. Working with several coaches and healers, the most impactful experience happened while he was living at a retreat centre.

In my own home, I metaphorically cut the cords between me and all my sons, releasing them to live their lives as independent adults. Hundreds of miles away, staff noticed a shift in my son's appearance, attitude, and behaviour. A few days later, I personally gave him a Gift of Independence, as much for me, as it was for him. I learned that to maintain my independence and respect theirs, I need to treat my adult sons like close friends. I love them, I am there for them and I let them live their own lives.

Cille Harris is a Facilitator from Ompah, Canada

Inspiration 107

"JUST"

Jo Plummer

Dear sisters in soul, why is it that you doubt your worth and right to equivalence? You see worthiness does not come from the 'thing' that you do. It comes from why and how you do them. Indeed, all of them. Cos' by the way, you are never 'just' one thing. Defining yourself singularly is only destined to one of two outcomes, that being failure or success. Your life is a bundle of 'things', some interrelated while others solitary.

What you do for work, be it paid or not, in or out of the home, with or without partners or children, full time or part time, in an office, shed, store, or even in the back bedroom, should not ever define your right to worth or equivalence. I so often hear you say I'm 'just' a …

Our interactions are rarely simultaneously firing on all four gas burners! Success is about the cumulative influence you have on others, from each and every interaction across all the 'things' that you do.

So next time you measure your own success, ask yourself whether your overall influence has been positive. You are worthy, you are equivalent and you are not 'just' anything … You ARE!

*Jo Plummer is a Business Owner
from Melbourne, Australia*

Inspiration 108

Reconnecting to the Goddess Within

Maria Jesus Romero (MariPosa)

When you reconnect to the goddess within it feels like returning 'home' to a sisterhood where strength, courage, love, and family bond you. The goddess is Gaia, the Grandmother Moon, Mother Nature. She is all living creatures, in every breath we take. A source of life, worshiped as the principal deity in various religions.

A goddess is a woman who emerges from deep within herself. She is a woman who has honestly explored her darkness and has learned to celebrate her light, as she can see the importance of embracing both sides because one cannot exist without the other. A goddess has both feminine and masculine energies, yin and yang, the sun and the moon, creating a harmonious balance with no separation between us, we are ONE. A goddess is able to fall in love with possibilities, and trust that all will be perfect in divine timing. She is just as willing to receive as she is to give, she fills her own cup for herself and overflows it for others.

"Never forget that YOU are a goddess and where there is a goddess, there is magic."

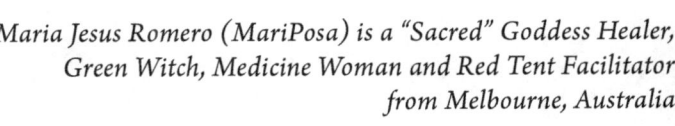

Maria Jesus Romero (MariPosa) is a "Sacred" Goddess Healer,
Green Witch, Medicine Woman and Red Tent Facilitator
from Melbourne, Australia

Inspiration 109

Joy

How do I feel when I am feeling joyful?

How am I going to include more of that into each and every day of my life?

Inspiration 110

My Paradise on This Earth

Leanne Swainson

When I was 25, I began a journey that would change my life forever: moving to the Central Australian Desert. I resided in the township of Yulara which is 20kms from Uluru (Ayers Rock). Nothing could prepare me for the way this place, with its landscape and colours, raw in beauty and unspoiled lands would have such an impact on my life. For the very first time, I felt at home in this world. I was blessed to be able to wake up to the backdrop of Uluru outside the lounge room window, to be surrounded by the bluest skies, rich rust coloured earth and green bushland that can only be found in the desert.

I found my passion for creativity whilst living in Central Australia which encouraged me to create textile art inspired by that beautiful place and the memories created there that I hold so dear. This by far would be one of the most memorable times in my life.

I hope I can inspire you to explore, travel, be spontaneous, live your life to the fullest and you too might find your place in this world.

Leanne Swainson is a Holistic Therapist, Reiki Master and Textile Artist from Medowie, NSW, Australia

Inspiration 111

My Challenges, My Inspiration

Mercy Mugure

Some of the truest and most admirable success stories are born in the darkest of places. And, they draw their inspiration and strength from God and summon courage within.

At the age of 10, I was diagnosed with a bone marrow infection that led to my current physical disability. My childhood took a different turn, from an active social life to being bedridden for many months that eventually turned to 12 years of medication. My already devastating situation was worsened by our cultural setting; my sickness was associated to witchcraft and punishment from gods.

I grew up knowing I was different. Haunted by more questions than answers. I never stopped wondering why among all my peers, and family members, why this bacterium had to pick on me.

But now I know why: I am the strong woman who deserved the disability because I could handle the challenges that came with it. Here I am a woman whose painful experiences are today's inspiration for the *Ability Africa Magazine* that goes beyond inspiring and changing the society's perspective on disability issues, BUT a key voices for the people with disabilities.

Mercy Mugure is a Linguistic Teacher from Westland, Nairobi

Inspiration 112

OMG! It's About Me!

Kerry Upham

Who would want to know about me? I spent much of my life hiding, being bullied and not fitting in. My truth, deep inside me, knew that I was not worthy, not deserving of the good stuff like friends and love.

I now know why I didn't fit. I experienced the world differently to those around me. I was a highly sensitive child; some might call me an empath. My sensitivity had me feeling other's emotions as clearly as if they were my own. I saw things others had no awareness of. I survived by shutting myself down.

To hell and back – what a journey of discovery, unraveling the mysteries of me.

I continue daily to face my fears and live in the light on the other side.

Growing personal awareness. Using meditation, mindfulness and self-nurturing to hold my self-love in place. Knowing love from the inside ensures I always am love. From my sensitivity curse, I have discovered the beauty of my gift and with that the beauty of myself.

Quote: Hold the vision, trust the process ~ Jenette Youngman

Kerry Upham is a Completions Practitioner; Coach; Counselor; Speaker; and Co-Author from Melbourne, Australia

Embracing Change

Ingrid Stump

A woman's place is in the kitchen. In my case, kitchens all over the world. My husband relocates for work, and as the trailing spouse, it falls on me to build a home, a safe haven.

I've done this eight times in our sixteen-year marriage. With excitement, trepidation, anger and sometimes downright hopelessness. When the excitement wears off, you find yourself in a strange country, where you don't know a soul, don't have a doctor or dentist, and most importantly, no HAIRDRESSER!

As many trailing spouses can attest to, it can be soul-destroying to start over again. It's like Groundhog Day! It can test and strain the bonds of even the strongest relationship. Every day brings its own challenges. But we persevere. There comes a time when we have to step up, dig deep and just get out there and do it! Whatever 'it' may be.

And one day, you realise it's okay. There's much to be grateful for. Family, togetherness, love, and the many friendships we have gathered all over the world. These thoughts keep me going. One step at a time. With humor and grace, and if I'm lucky, a glass of champagne in my hand.

Ingrid Stump is an Administrator from Skipton, England

Inspiration 114

Step into the Extraordinary

Liesel Albrecht

Retreats change lives – they just do – I have seen it, felt it and basked in its glory. I believe that by taking time to step from our ordinary lives into something extraordinary then we can truly understand who we are and reconnect with the deepest parts of us that sometimes stays hidden.

I have learnt that on a retreat you get to take time just for you and you get to listen to that whisper in your ear, the whisper that urges change. The one that you ignore until you can ignore it no longer. There is something about this experience that truly does provide a transformational and magical experience where life can change in an instant. I felt this magic on a retreat to Mexico where I got to walk the paths of Mayan Goddesses, and I spent time with women who truly understood what it was like to feel and reconnect with themselves, for me it was significant as it taught me that it is when we listen that something magical takes place – something that allows us to walk the path we are meant to be walking and become truly happy.

Liesel Albrecht is The Retreat Specialist from Traralgon, Australia

Inspiration 115

Love is the Answer

Cheryl Campbell

When we give birth to our children we often daydream about the life we want for them. A happy, healthy life filled with the least number of struggles as possible. When I had my son I too had dreams for his life and not one of them was, I want him to grow up and be addicted to drugs, lose 20 kilos and turn into an angry person. That was the path he chose to take and as a parent the frustration, anxiety, guilt and overwhelming sadness that I felt on a daily basis was paralysing.

During the seven years of his addiction I tried many things to get him off drugs. I yelled, screamed, cried, ignored and had panic attacks. It took me a long time to realise to help him all I had to do was be his mum and love him unconditionally. Loving someone unconditionally doesn't mean you must like what they are doing, instead love the person that you know is buried deep inside them and is struggling to get out.

My son went to rehab and has been clean for over two years and thanks me often for being his mum and loving him unconditionally.

Cheryl Campbell is a Mentor, Inspirational Speaker and Author from Melbourne, Australia

Education Makes a Difference

Milka Roach

It's impossible to learn, thrive and grow while you are in fear and your only focus is survival. This was my reality for the first half of my life. Like too many women, I was stuck in a violent relationship. As a young migrant, I didn't have enough knowledge to find a way out. I survived each day, just for my children. Eventually, I escaped that relationship, but I was no longer the vibrant young woman I had been.

In time, work and a supportive partner gave me the confidence I needed to take the next leap: education. I enrolled in a childcare course especially for people from non-English backgrounds. Studying and learning opened up a whole new world to me.

It's now 27 years since I graduated. I have established two award-winning OOSH services and I also opened a multicultural resource centre. In 2015 I was nominated for the Australian of the Year award for community involvement.

If you are afraid, ask for help. There is a way out. If you know someone is in need, extend your hand. Being free from fear gave me a new life. Education gave me a new world.

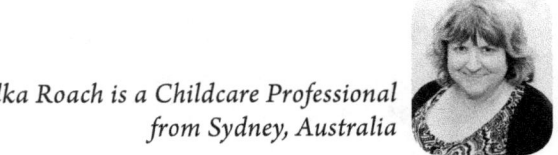

Milka Roach is a Childcare Professional from Sydney, Australia

Inspiration 117

Love

Ten things that I most love about my life and myself.

Be Inspired by Change

Hazel Theocharous

There have been two miracles in my life so far: my two wonderful children. This experience has made me realise the value of life and how important it is to see the joy again in everything which surrounds you on a daily basis through their eyes.

Dynamics in your life change once you have a child and it can sometimes feel that there is no longer any time for you or what you feel you were destined to do or achieve. But by including the needs of your children and family into your new life, you discover and realise that your achievements have only just begun and you have new goals.

I worked in a corporate environment until my first son was school age, managing my life and work around him until that point, through all of that time realising that goal posts were changing and so was I. But it was when I saw my life through my five year old child's eyes and his longing for time with me, that the values in my life really changed – it was time to stop and start anew. My own business career began and so did the next achievements in my life. It does take a lot of hard work to change your goals and values, but when you do, you realise that the joy and happiness you bring to your family and your life makes it all worth while.

Hazel Theocharous is a Small Business Coach and Trainer from London, United Kingdom

Transformation Life by Design

Faye Waterman

As a woman in the third act of life I am finding life to be really amazing. It has taken me over three decades to find the real me, to have the courage to pursue my life's purpose and passion.

A journey that has been one not too different to most of you, there have been many ups and downs, the successes and the failures, but the one thing I have never done is give up when the going gets tough. Never allowing the negative chatter or opinions of others to prevent me from pursuing my dreams.

I have always known that my life's purpose depended on my certainty, courage and strength to pursue my dreams, regardless of what negative chatter gets in my way.

Ever since I can remember I have known that my path in life is to be a transformational speaker and author to inspire and create certainty and hope for women. Educating the masses, particularly children from in the younger years of their lives, creating awareness and a voice, so they can be a stronger and more courageous next generation. Certainty, courage, strength.

"Alone we can do so little; together we can do so much." – Helen Keller

Faye Waterman is a Radio Producer from Melbourne, Australia

Inspiration 120

Choices and My Mother

Natalya Stefanac

Your choices determine your destiny. There's only one person who can choose for yourself and that is you. I can't turn back the time and change anything from the past, but I can change my future. Be careful of your choices. Remember your choices lead to your destiny. I want to make the right choices, be happy and have the best life.

A mother holds her child's hand for a short time but holds their heart forever.

My mum inspires me a lot and I look up to her. My mum's job is to inspire and help me learn. It makes me feel happy that I will hold onto my mum's hand along the way. I know she REALLY loves me. No matter where I am, I know my mum will always be there for me. Even though I haven't had the best life and I swap houses (alternate week with each parent), my mum's love grows bigger. When I see her, she always gives me a hug.

One day, in a long time to come, my mum will pass away, but I know that my mum is in my heart and I will always think of her.

Natalya Stefanac is a Student from Melbourne, Australia

Fix Your Focus

Emily Farmer

Failure to believe that we are nothing but capable and incredible is what stands between us and our goals, it's what makes greatness so hard to achieve. If you are fearful of failure, If you have a line of backup plans waiting for you to fall back on because you don't see your ambition pulling through, you aren't leaping high enough to reach your dream. The degree of success you reach is solely determined by the expectations that you set for yourself so don't let anything hold you back.

The belief that we are not good enough is why we fail, so don't be afraid of going all in to achieve your goals, be expectant that you will conquer, be confident that you are ready. By putting time and energy into self doubt or hesitation you are putting your purpose at stake, if you don't back down, if you don't stop short, it will happen, faith in your goals doesn't take away the fear, it shows us how to fight it.

With your focus fixed and your heart expectant for individual greatness you are set to conquer and achieve your goals. Keep moving forward, keep moving towards your ambition, don't let fear be what stops you. Your hope knows how to bounce back from rock bottom so don't be afraid of stumbling along the way.

Emily Farmer is a Student from Melbourne, Australia

Inspiration 122

You are Resilient

Samara Egglezos

"The human capacity for burden is like bamboo – far more flexible than you'd ever believe at first glance."
– Jodi Picoult, Resilience

What is resilience? Google, define resilience: The capacity to recover quickly from difficulties; toughness. We are all going to have rough times in our lives. It's like a road trip. Some parts will be bumpy, others will be smooth and calming. Sometimes we have to accept the negativity to see the positive side in things. Everything will be easier if you stay strong. Although, I know sometimes it's hard. To me, it's easy to cry, and that's okay. Being emotional is absolutely normal. As long as we don't lose control. Because that's where it starts to gets hard. Think of it this way: when you lose yourself in a maze, it's hard to find a way out; When you lose control crying, it's hard to stop. Most of the time, all we need is to take a deep breath. Keep calm, and carry on.

Samara Egglezos is a Student from Melbourne, Australia

Inspiration 123

My Purpose

I know my purpose in life is …

Inspiration 124

Now Choose Life

Cybelle Liporoni

In 1990 my husband and I moved from Brazil to Australia. Six months later, I understood why people called us brave.

It takes a lot of courage to leave your culture, family and possessions behind and start again in a country where you don't speak the language and have no friends. When the excitement was over I started to realise the costs of our choices. I felt depressed, discouraged and hopeless.

One day someone showed me a statement from the Bible: *"Now choose life, so that you and your children may live." (Deut 30:19)*

Something inside me started to re-connect to the values I had lost. One of my values was my faith in the Living God – Jesus. I started reading the Bible and looked for a church to help me understand the Word of God better. I regained my confidence in who I am in Christ and how much God loves me. I activated the power of the Holy Spirit in me and went after the plans and purposes God has for my life. Today I am fully restored, full of life and helping others who had forgotten how special they are.

We are all special to God. His Spirit gives us the tools we need to recognise and use the gifts we already have.

Cybelle Liporoni is a Physiotherapist, Counsellor, SRE Teacher and Missionary from Australia.

Inspiration 125

Be Strong

Laura Stuettgen

An important lesson I have learnt over the last few years is to appreciate and learn from the inspiring women in my life. It has taken me some time to come to appreciate the strong, smart women I am surrounded with everyday – from my mother, to my cousins, aunts, colleagues and girlfriends.

It is comforting to know that if I ever need a shoulder to cry on or advice, there will always be someone for me to lean on. There is always strength and guidance right on my door step should I need it. No need to look outside of your circle of friends and family to find inspiration.

One of my favourite quotes has rung true of past few years: "Strong women – may we know them, may we raise them, may we be them." I hope that, for the rest of my life, I will be surrounded by strong, capable and inspirational women, (one day) raise them, and in turn, be one.

Laura Stuettgen is a Recruitment Consultant from Melbourne, Australia

I Love Myself

Melissa Groom

I used to hate myself. I used to feel dirty. I carried hurt from my childhood into my adult life like a wounded soldier. People told me to let it go, that 'it' was in the past. I meditated, exercised, detoxed, cleansed, wrote in my journal, read books, attended seminars, watched motivational videos, repeated positive affirmations, did visualizations, went to healers, went on retreats, drank, smoked, self-harmed to numb the pain, cried, screamed and yelled.

Some days I wished that tomorrow I would not wake up because I could never rid myself of this disgusting feeling that I defined as 'me'. I could not get rid of the feeling that I was not good enough to be loved, to be protected, or to be pure.

I created a story about myself that I was 'dirty' because of what someone did to me. I allowed it to rob me of so much happiness, self-confidence, self-worth, and self-love. After completing Louise Hay's course, *You Can Heal Your Life*, I learnt that I am not my story or what happened to me.

I love myself just the way I am. I am beautiful!

Melissa Groom is a Business Mentor from Kingscliff NSW, Australia

Autumn (Fall) Equinox

Emma Sidney

Just as in the spring, the equinox is a moment of equal day and night. This is a time to give thanks for the summer and be ready for the coming darkness. It's the time of harvest, of counting one's blessings, of meditation on what can be left behind, and what needs to stay.

The traditions around equinoxes are worldwide and there are many ways of remembering this moment of balance. Pagans have Mabon, the second harvest. Japan calls both equinoxes Ohigan, which is a time to meditate, and visit relatives and ancestral graves. The moon festival is a lunar tradition in Asia and the USA, where celebrations include gazing at the moon, and moon cakes or moon pies are consumed. Archangels are also heralded as 'Michaelmas', for Archangel Michael is celebrated. The light is now going to fade, the leaves are falling and the earth is cooling. Turn your mind inwards to focus on what will sustain you through the coming months.

Review what works for you and what doesn't. What can you study, refine or eliminate, as indoors replaces out? Write down what serves you now and what will you have the energy for, as the weather gets colder and the light wanes. Consider your food, remember sustaining meals and walk outside to adjust to the cold gently. As the dark grows, find your light inside. Autumn (Fall) equinox is approximately on 20-22 March. (This is spring in the northern hemisphere.)

Emma Sidney is a Business Owner and Copywriter from Melbourne, Australia

Old History, New History

Desiree Blaich

"Step out of the history that is holding you back. Step into the new story you are willing to create."
– Oprah Winfrey

This quote really struck a chord with me. I'd spent way too long stuck in the history of my mistakes and suffering terribly from them. They held me back for years. I was bitter, angry, frustrated and just couldn't get past it. I felt like I had been cursed with a terrible fate and nothing I did would change that. The blame I put on myself and others weighed me down. I couldn't forgive those who had hurt me and it was a huge burden to carry. I wasn't a happy person and I felt I couldn't trust anyone. It was a lonely and sad place to be and it didn't get me anywhere with such a bad attitude. I hit rock bottom and knew that if I didn't do anything about it, nothing would change. Something had to be done and only I could do it.

So I created a new story. I surrounded myself with positive people, mainly my family, and started doing things that I enjoyed again. I humbled myself and I forgave those who had done me wrong. Most importantly I forgave myself. It didn't change overnight, but gradually over time my life changed for the better. I had faith and hope; a belief that God would help if I did my part. And He did.

I don't live the perfect life and I still have plenty of challenges, but I have created a new story, full of happiness, faith and hope for the future.

Desiree Blaich is a Teacher from Melbourne, Australia

Inspiration 129

Let Your Feminine Empress Rise!

Jonita D'Souza

It's been a long time coming
This emergence, this awakening
This undeniable fire
Building up in my soul.
It's been a muted existence
This acting, pretending
I believed my charade
Trying to please them all.
I believed that the shadow
That sought out acceptance
Survived on approval
And shrouded in guilt.
Deserved nothing more than
A tirade of rejections
Wasn't worth a stitch more
Than the emptiness I felt.
I was wrong.

A Feminine Empress was born
Encased in this body
Her spirit is strong
As love returned it revealed
My beauty and emotions
Dreams and desires
That were here all along
And I grew strong.

A Feminine Empress was nurtured
Ancient wisdoms reconnected
An essence I thought gone.
Trusting daily my body's
Strengths and intuition,
Mother Earth and the Sisterhood
Guiding my intimate love
And finally I am ready.
A Feminine Empress is rising.

Sensuality and pleasure,
Life's gifts I embrace.
Standing in my power
Vulnerable and brave
I see fellow sisters
Rising to do the same.
And so it is! Here we are.
Our truth has been waiting
We've only to embrace
It is time, Sisters
Let your Feminine Empress Rise!

Jonita D'Souza is a Feminine Lifestyle Expert and Author from London, United Kingdom

Inspiration 130

Letting Go

Five things I am willing to let go of starting today.

Inspiration 131

Be Yourself

Natalya Stefanac

"When you feel copied, remember that people can only go where you have already been. They have no idea where you are going next."
– Liz Lange

I have learnt many things and even though I'm 11, people copy me all the time. They don't have any idea what I'm going to do next. Sometimes you can show people and if they copy you it can also be a compliment. They still can't have the success you have now, they can only follow right where you've been. They are not going to get anywhere.

My advice would be to make your own path. Don't always copy others, stand out and be different. Be yourself and if that means doing something different to others, it doesn't matter. Wear your own skin. You only live once. So make it count.

Natalya Stefanac is a Student from Melbourne, Australia

Inspiration 132

For Life is a Journey

Susan Maslin

Since I was a teenager I have carried in my purse a scrap of paper with these words from T.S. Eliot's Four Quartets. I have found them inspirational. At times when I have needed support and guidance I have reread these lines… for life is a journey with its ups and downs.

Our journey is to discover more about our world, about life, about ourselves, about the mysteries of the universe and we are therefore always learning along the way.

This lifelong journey of exploration and the goal of the exploring is not so much to reach the destination or come to explain all the mysteries, so to speak, but to arrive where we started and know the place for the first time through new eyes and new understanding.

> *"We shall not cease from exploration*
> *And the end of all our exploring*
> *Will be to arrive where we started*
> *And know the place for the first time."*

Susan Maslin is President of Soroptimist International from Melbourne Australia

Have No Regrets

Katerina Egglezos

"I'd rather regret the things I've done than regret the things I haven't done."
– Lucille Ball

In life we go through many challenges and face many obstacles along the way. We may sometimes try to avoid things so that we don't have regrets in the future. However, we may regret the things we haven't done but should have done. Life is too short for regrets and we should all make the most out of life. It doesn't matter about the amount of mistakes that we make along the way. Mistakes are a part of life.

We learn and grow from our mistakes, not letting them hold us back but moving forward to bigger, better and greater things. Life is about learning, taking risks and being adventurous. Being open to new opportunities and doing things differently because with hard work, there are no limits. Don't let anything or anyone hold you back, because in the end, the regrets you are going to have are for the things you didn't do.

Katerina Egglezos is a Student from Melbourne, Australia

Inspiration 134

Are You Serious?

Sheridan Morris

Do you take your business seriously? Do you think that means you must ALWAYS appear "professional" and "business-like"? Are you taking seriousness too seriously? Do you allow time for fun and laughter?

I've always had a keen sense of humour and found that integrating it into my business helped me to build my success. To engage prospects and retain customers, you need to be memorable. Developing and using your sense of humour in your communications gets them smiling and laughing, and anchors your name and business in their minds.

Taking my humour seriously and learning the structures and formulas of comedy, gave me the confidence and courage to perform in the Melbourne International Comedy Festival and at stand-up gigs. When I travelled the long, dark journey of depression, I found that actively practicing my sense of humour helped me to feel better and regain my well-being.

Tap into the power of humour in your daily routine and your business practices. Look for funny things around you, share silly stories, and get your customers and team laughing with you.

Lift your spirits, renew your energy and boost your body with curative, enlivening serotonin through laughter. Life is too short to be serious!

Sheridan Morris is a Professional Writer from Melbourne, Australia

Inspiration 135

Unfiltered Truth

Brenda Dempsey

I have found the missing piece of my jigsaw puzzle! It is mind blowing! It is beyond my imagination yet it is simple, clear and true. You know when someone talks, and you just get it? You just get them? Everything makes perfect sense ...

It scares you but you are like a moth to the flame ... you can't help but be attracted to it even though it's terrifying. You succumb to the fear ... yes, fear! It's time to kick all FEAR into touch. It does not exist except in your mind.

Can you touch fear? NO! Can you smell fear? NO! Can you taste fear? NO!

You feel fear? Yes but that's because you talk yourself into it. It's the negative energy that resides in you. The negative energy blocks all light and positive energy in you that creates everything you desire ...

Be fearless ... You have the power ... Flick the switch! Yet fear always blocks the action, so how do you rid yourself of it? Speak UNFILTERED TRUTH!

I have found my Queen ... You can too ... It's time to take the lead in your life ... It's time to be transformed ...

It's time to be Super Conscious YOU!

Brenda Dempsey is an Energetic Coach
from Surrey, England

Inspiration 136

What If?

Maike Sundmacher

What if today was different? What if today you believed it was possible? What if today you thought you could?

What if, for just one day, you gave yourself permission to be you, to believe, to love and to live … the way you want to, the way you deserve, wholeheartedly. What if today was that day?

What would you do? How would you feel and what would you accomplish? Who would you be if you forgot the 'shoulds', dumped the 'musts', and ditched the 'have tos'? What if – instead – you embraced your inspiration, your purpose, your passion, your path? What if today you gently closed your eyes, listened to your heart, tapped into your intuition and visualised your new life? And what if today was the day you stepped into your power and committed to it, fully?

How would your life unfold if you made that decision today? What if you made the same choice tomorrow, and every day after that? What if your courage today inspired the women around you tomorrow?

Embracing my forward-looking 'what if' was scary; yet, even scarier would have been to look back and ask, 'what if?'

What if … ?

Maike Sundmacher is a Mindset Coach, Author and Trainer from Sydney, Australia

Don't Quit

Tracey Hall

This has been a motto for me for many a decade. Why, you ask? Well, a long time ago a friend said, 'You are a quitter because you gave up doing that childcare course.' This stuck with me, because I didn't want to be a quitter, but I also didn't want to be in a job that I would hate.

Nothing about that job appealed to me and now being over 40 I know why. I never wanted to be a mother, but have been blessed with three children and one grandchild now. I didn't think I would do a good job as my mother was such a terrible one (yes, I know it sounds hurtful, but she was). Ironically she died ten years ago this year and I don't miss her as much as my friend who died the same year.

My friend didn't have a choice, she was murdered. YES, family violence had touched me as a young child and now as an adult it touched me again. It made me realise even though she was gone she is never forgotten. Always remember those who have touched your lives.

Tracey Hall is a Mentor/Trainer for Direct Sales Industry from Melbourne, Australia

Inspiration 138

Inspiration

Ten words that have inspired me from reading this book.

Finding Joy Through Grief

Vicki McClifty

"The way through sadness and grief that comes from great loss is to use it as motivation and to generate a deeper sense of purpose"
– the Dalai Lama

My son's passing was a true test of my faith in the Universe. There is no greater battle. Survival will make you stronger. How we respond to our experience determines our future. From a positive stance, such loss generates a deeper sense of purpose in your life. For me, I found motivation to fulfil my son's life-long pursuit of happiness. Slowly shifting focus from my own grief onto helping others, lessened my own burden. Joy evolved.

If you have travelled this torturous path, my heart aches for you. Take your time to grieve. Feel your loss. You are not alone in your suffering. Your life has profoundly changed forever. Be kind to yourself. Be open about your grief. Slowly, you will emerge appreciating your world on a deeper and more meaningful level. You will discover your authenticity, your soul's purpose. With your loved one always guiding you in spirit, I urge you to take the high road and choose to make your journey a joyous ride for two!

Vicki McClifty is a Life Enhancement Coach, AM Healing My Soul from Brisbane, Australia

Inspiration 140

Take Your Own Advice

Josie Kearsey

What advice would you give your 20 year old self? I would tell you not to be guided by other people's influence, not to think that their opinion is the be all and end all, and for you to not shape your life based on their opinion. In your life, you have what you desire. What is your passion and the driving force behind what makes you 'you'? Your life is like a canvas for you to paint on; choose the colours that reflect your dreams, your desires and your passion.

I would tell you to not fret or fear, even though you are young. Be bold, step out and do the things that your soul is convicting you to do. You may look back one day and say, 'I wish I'd have listened to my inner voice, my own instinct and intuition.' I am saying this because this is my truth. Living in regret is not an option unless you make it one. I have instilled this in my daughter, to make her own decisions about love, life and career. I know that she has blossomed and become the person she has always desired to be. I just wish someone had let me be me and not coloured my world with their palette.

Josie Kearsey is an Event Director from Melbourne, Australia

If You're a Daughter

Robyn Harrison

If you're a daughter, be proud of what you learn and teach. It doesn't matter where you came from or whether or not you know where you're going. What does matter is that you belong to an incredibly exclusive club. One where all members deserve respect, and the right to be who they truly are.

When the gift of a daughter is given to us, we write a story based on our own lives from the moment we look into those beautiful eyes. We don't get a manual to guide us through the growing years; we never stop growing and nor do they.

So be proud of your story, and be proud of what you teach your daughters, even when you think they have rewritten the story you wrote that first day. Because if you read between the lines, they have just embellished their story with what they've learned along their path and what you've taught them while travelling yours.

Robyn Harrison is an Artist and Teacher from Sydney, Australia

Inspiration 142

Hope and Intuition

Birgit Schwitalla

"There is no way to peace, peace is the way."
– Mahatma Gandhi

The desire for peace begins in myself
if I'm tired being constantly in a kind of war

I was looking for my inner peace
found it finally in my heart
accepted me as who I am
and now peace is growing roots in me
finally no more war

no more power-struggle
no more comparisons and condemn to anything or anyone
accepting things as they are

"It is like it is
and it comes as it comes"
… this ancient River-Rhine wisdom of my grandmother
and my father's motto as well
accompanied me my entire life
and now finally ended up in me

I send a smile in my environment
and my enviroment smiles back to me
give it a try

only willing to see and learn the good
based on my intuition and my good experiences

I'm landed
where I was already in my childhood
in the abundance of the good
supported by my hope
coming home to my longing

peaceful in love – with me
a very personal, daily, intuitive inspiration

*Birgit Schwitalla is a Stylist
from Düsseldorf, Germany*

Inspiration 143

Focus

I am choosing to focus on more of what I love rather than what I cannot control.
Here is my list of five things I choose to focus on today.

Flawsome Heroine

Ana Bogdanovska

In every story there is a hero and a there is a villain. The hero or heroine are embodying the highest values like bravery, courage and justice.

The heroine struggles to reach the truth and wants nothing for herself, everything that she does is for the others. The heroine is required to be perfect, flawless, because flaws make her an ordinary person, and a heroine in the eyes of the others can't be an ordinary woman.

A heroine must never give up, she must to be prepared to face any danger, any disappointment, any defeat, a heroine can never give up her fight. We are all heroines, but not in some fairytale story, but in a real life where every day we have to fight and to be strong.

Instead for everybody expecting us to be flawless and perfect they should know that we are awesome because of our flaws. So my dear ladies, love yourself, respect yourself and most importantly accept yourself the way you are.

Don't be afraid to be the heroine of your own life, because you already are! A FLAWSOME one! (Flaws + awesome= Flawsome – Tyra Banks' phrase)

Ana Bogdanovska is a Master of Laws LL.M. from Skopje, Republic of Macedonia

Inspiration 145

Test Yourself

Farisai Dzemwa (Joymore)

If life has swept the floors with you, if the world has attacked you head on, if your own heart has ached so much until it feels like it has eaten all your insides up, if pain has numbed your responses and your senses somewhat and yet still each morning you wake up willing to put up a good fight with whatever life throws at you, God is trying to say something to you: He ain't done with you yet. There is a bigger picture/revelation in construction. All your experiences will equip you for the bigger picture and will come in handy. Look unto Him and embrace His holy spirit so you might be able to receive your calling and work with it until His desires are fulfilled. Only then can we sing Hosanna to the highest! So, woman of integrity, never give up or give in, but embrace every situation as it will help you discover the strength and courage within.

You will never know how far you can go until you take up the journey. You will never know the extent of your own strength until you put it to the test.

Farisai Dzemwa (Joymore) is a Mental Health Nurse and Mentor from Wolverhampton, United Kingdom

Inspiration 146

Be ACE!

Heather Schmidt

A word I say regularly is "ACE". Three words I love and try to live by are: Awareness, Curiosity, Equality. The world becomes less hostile and more friendly when we adopt being "ACE". Get curious, become self aware and judge less. We are all created equally. One thing that sets some apart from others is belief. When you have limiting beliefs and fears you limit yourself. When you have a belief system with a foundation of positivity and possibility you are more inclined to try new things, look on the bright side and be more resilient. We project our beliefs on others too. Think of the last time you looked at someone and created an assumption or belief for them. "He has no shoes on, he must be poor." "Her hair is messy, she's been out all night." "She looks angry, what a miserable girl."

Get curious, notice your judgment and ask yourself, what could their story be? Without asking them you'll never know. Could you be more kind and empathetic in your judgement? Like this, "That guy must love the feeling of sand between his toes." "This girl is loving life so much she forgot to do her hair this morning." "She's going over her exam notes in her head I hope she passes."

Everyone deserves respect. We never know someone's inside story unless we ask. You may even stop and start up a conversation. BE ACE

Heather Schmidt is a Nature Direct Consultant from Melbourne Australia

Do What You Love

Melitta Hardenberg

I remember when I was young I used to spend hours dreaming what my future would hold and how I would live my full potential. When I was seven I believed in myself. I certainly never imagined I'd end up collapsing in a heap physically, mentally, and emotionally. I don't know when the self-doubt crept in but it did, and it was paralyzing.

Fast-forward seven years and now I run my own business, have two beautiful daughters, a loving husband and a circle of support that rocks my world. What I learnt between then and now can be summarized by this:

- Do what you love and never compromise. Do what makes your heart sing.
- Build daily self-care habits that fill your cup such as moving or reading.
- Find a good friend who makes you laugh … and laugh often.
- Find an unreasonable friend who doesn't let you off the hook. She's the one who makes you run in the rain knowing you'll feel better after!
- Do something that scares you just a little bit, but not too much. Happiness does indeed live just outside of your comfort zone.

We all have a voice of doubt, my advice… thank her for her input and rock out your best self.

Melitta Hardenberg is a Health and Wellness Coach from Melbourne, Australia

Inspiration 148

I Am

*Twenty powerful "I Am" statements that I will read each day
out loud to inspire me and lift my self-belief.*

Inspiration 149

Trust Yourself

Yukiko Mukumoto Ruthford

I was born and raised in Kyoto Japan. When I was 15 years old, I left home for three years to attend high school in New Zealand. This was a life changing experience. Meeting new friends from many different countries opened my eyes to see that there are so many different cultures, languages and beliefs. All these kinds of differences that I wouldn't have experienced if I had only lived in Japan. While I was living away from my family, I learned as long as I choose the right path, most things in life will turn out alright. Sometimes, when negativity takes over and I don't even have a tiny little space in my mind to think of the simple direction I want to go in life, it has somehow always ended up alright.

Now, I live in Australia with my husband and two sons. I'm still learning many things, not just cultural differences but school systems, different lifestyles and education policies within families, including within my own household. Since I married, I learned that I cannot control who people are just like they cannot control me, even if they are closely connected with me. When I expect too much sometimes I get let down as I'm only expecting the good.

So, have a clean conscience and don't let others make you second guess yourself. Enjoy your life everyday because the day you spend now will never come back to you. There is no magic to making life better, but you have unlimited power to do so. Go with the flow, don't worry and trust yourself to be alright.

*Yukiko Mukumoto Ruthford is a Mother
from Brisbane, Australia*

Sister Since Six

Samantha Goss

"Though no one can go back and make a brand new start, anyone can start from now and make a brand new ending."
– Carl Bard

From the age of six we knew we would create something amazing together. Healing the world may not quite have been what we had in mind, although it is our intention now! We have always shared our personal holistic health experiences with others and Soul Health Seeker has organically grown from that. We give the gift of Direction, Hope, Health and Growth like we did in Eliza's case. She is now 20 and had suffered from anxiety and depression since the age of 15, she was anorexic, self-harming, on antidepressants and had just survived a suicide attempt. We helped resolve her underlying issues and she now has a more positive belief system. She views food differently, has put on weight, is off medication, obtained her licence, gained employment and no longer self-harms or suffers from anxiety and depression.

This reinforced what we always knew; that there are life changing, medication free ways to find Direction, Hope, Health, and Growth.

Samantha Goss is a Business Owner from Blairgowrie, Australia

Inspiration 151

Avoid Distraction & Focus on Action

Melanie Parker

The happy, content and successful woman is someone who takes action by staying focused and avoids distraction at all cost. Edith Armstrong describes her vision in life as wanting to create a life full of peace, harmony, health, love and abundance, she says, "I keep my mind focused on peace, harmony, health, love and abundance. Then, I can't be distracted by doubt, anxiety, or fear."

The very word DISTRACTION contains the word ACTION. Distraction takes us off purpose. Today's world has more distractions waiting to lure us than any other time before. We must develop laser-focus on our heart's desires if we want to succeed in living our best life. Let's tear away the DISTR-action and get back to only focusing on the ACTION that will increase our happiness and take us from a feeling of discontent to becoming inspired and successful in life, business and play!

What're your heart's desires? What action can you choose to take today to keep your mind focused on living your life's purpose? The life you imagined is waiting for you … Choose success today!

Melanie Parker is a Trainer of Direct Sales and Personal Development from Sydney, Australia

Have High Standards

Rachpal Tulsi

If anyone suggested to me when I was a little girl that my work will be a departure from the standard 9 to 5, six days a week, I would have probably laughed at them. It was a different time, where going to university was a dream for many women and becoming a secretary, a nurse or a salesgirl was the norm.

Now almost 30 years since I left school at 18, I not only have a Master's Degree, but for the last 15 years, I've moved from a full-time job to being a consultant and now even lecturing at university. I've travelled around the Asia-Pacific region for my work and when I don't have projects, I work from home.

One can only dream lofty dreams. I am probably my own biggest competitor, challenging myself to achieve the high goals I set and often dwelling in uncertainty. In the face of obstacles, I create new paths and new opportunities. And just like my heels, I always keep my standards high.

Rachpal Tulsi is an Organisation Development Consultant, Coach and Lecturer from Singapore

Inspiration 153

Finding My Way

Joanne Golias

They say you cannot change the past but you can learn from it. In my early twenties I had everything a woman could desire. Then everything changed. I was facing major heartbreak with the betrayal of my husband. Two and half years later I divorced – I was shattered, vulnerable and broken. I resigned from my job with the National Australia Bank and was disillusioned.

In my early Thirties I was working in hospitality and did some Personal Assistant jobs. Instead of getting on with life I was 'stuck' with the inability to move-on. In my late Thirties I got a job at a Five Star Gentlemen's Club as a Manager. It is within this environment that I found comfort and realised how wonderfully blessed I was. In my early Forties I become a Director of this Club whilst being Manager On Duty.

A final sayonara to the past. I am now a Licensed Real Estate Agent and Auctioneer. I feel happy and fulfilled with all that I have achieved. I look forward to my Fabulous Fifties. I feel empowered, loved and have self respect.

It's time to start a fresh. Be bold and beautiful and to embrace my life and my future. This is dedicated to my mother and father and three sisters for their unconditional love and support.

Joanne Golias is in Real Estate from Melbourne, Australia

Blow Your Own Trumpet

Chris Dennis

Blow Your Own Trumpet is a quote from my nanna. A very strong willed woman who believed that girls and women can succeed at everything they want to. During my school years, I took this literally … I played a trumpet! This wasn't really what Nanna had meant.

In later years I learnt it was about being able to believe in myself in every part of my life. Giving myself permission to say, "I'm awesome in my business, I'm awesome with my personal relationships." In fact… I'm awesome full stop.

In most cultures women are taught to take a back seat and lessen their achievements, and not been seen to be a "Tall Poppy". Don't be scared to share. Your achievements are awesome. No matter how big or small, they are yours – be proud of your achievements.

Today is your day, in fact every day is your day to believe in your thoughts, your actions, your self and your life.

> Take time to believe and dream.
> Take time to be your awesome self.
> Take time to Blow Your Own Trumpet and let the world know who you are.

Chris Dennis is a Tender Management Specialist from Melbourne, Australia

Inspiration 155

Worthy Woman

Joanne Worthy

Dear worthy woman, Yes you, the woman reading this right now. You are beautiful beyond measure, You are unique and you were born to be magnificent. Please believe this.

Go deep and heal your wounds from the past, let go of the disappointments and betrayal. Heal and trust yourself so you can open your heart and your soul fully. Love yourself a little more each day to allow more love in and your life will be enriched with more abundance.

Embrace all that you are, imperfectly perfect. Allow yourself to be that amazing women you are destined to be and allow the universe to provide for you whilst you consciously create the life you dreamed of. Be kind, compassionate and loving, yet strong in your convictions. Be brave beautiful woman and do not allow fear to paralyse you from achieving everything you desire.

The universe is waiting for you to step up and be that women you were destined to be. You were born to be AMAZING, go shine your light and sprinkle your beauty around. Live your life with passion and meaning and allow yourself to truly love who you are. And may your life truly be a masterpiece.

*Joanne Worthy is a Coach
from Canberra, Australia*

Inspiration 156

Find Your Voice

Rhonda Brown

At 22 I had the fairytale wedding which turned into the honeymoon from hell. I'd married the man I thought was my Prince Charming only he turned out to be Mr Jekyll and Hyde. The many years of living with this kind of person soon took its toll. I sunk into depression. I'd lost my power, felt hopeless, totally invisible as a person. It became all about survival each day, barely functioning – and I feared for my girls.

After finding a small glimmer of strength, we fled and began a new life. The after effect was healing and releasing the repetitive thoughts that sabotaged living the desired new life. Feelings of not being quite good enough, invisible, not heard and trouble trusting myself to make decisions.

I'm passionate about helping women who've left a traumatic relationships to transform their life. Giving back their voice and power through art and creativity to heal, get back their voice and power to attract and make better choices for a full and free life.

This then flows on to their children and others to stop the cycle of women having their power stripped from them in traumatic relationships.

Rhonda Brown is a TV Host from Brisbane, Australia

Give and Be Blessed

Andrea Donaldson

Giving isn't always about giving financially. We can give of our time and our talents. We can give to others the gift of our full attention by listening closely. We can give by teaching someone a new skill and investing something of ourselves.

In giving we should be changed. We have tried to teach our kids, with the gifts that they've received – the blessing they've received in their life – comes an expectation, or a responsibility, to pass that on. Do not be a stagnant pool, but be a running brook. In other words, become a conduit for blessing, rather than trying to keep it all for yourself. Resources can come through us and go onto others. One of our daughters now sponsors a child herself through Compassion. She has been blessed to be a blessing.

Extracted from Andrea Donaldson's, *Travelling Home: A Flight Plan for the Journey to Joy.*

Andrea Donaldson is an Occupational Therapist and Business Coach from Melbourne, Australia

Get Back Up!

Ritu Sharma

Pain is the reason that we grow. While we sit in our comfort zone and admire the set-up around us, we fail to see the land of opportunity that we are on. We are looking for another piece of land, while there isn't one. It is the discomfort, the pain that shakes us and wakes us up.

Our evolution happens through pain. Until we learn the lessons we are supposed to learn, life keeps giving us one blow after the other. It pokes us, thrashes us and pulls and pushes us to re-shape our outlook. Sometimes, the process leaves permanent marks on our souls. But we evolve and we grow.

This is the reward! Life becomes good eventually because of the lessons we have learnt and the pain we have endured and the acceptance we have developed of ourselves along the journey. Once the lesson has been learnt, there isn't a chance of making the same mistakes again. We are eventually, firmly grounded. Pain is the road to evolution and falling is a part of the growth process.

When it knocks you down, get back up!

> Stand taller!
> Mightier!
> Stronger!
> More of YOU each time!

Ritu Sharma is a Teacher, Inspirational Speaker and Entrepreneur from Walsall, England

Inspiration 159

Everyone Has Their Own Story

Colleen Roberts

True diamonds go through a rigorous process that shape and mould them to show their best potential. The same can be said for us as girls and later as women. Some have an easy path, some have a hard path. When I used to compare my life to my friends and other people I felt hard done by, but when I compared it to others less fortunate I felt blessed and grateful.

When my children were young I used to say a little prayer or affirmation. It was, "As long as my children are healthy, and I am healthy we will get by." That is what I lived by. My children and myself have always had good health and got by and for that I am most grateful.

Your health, your spirit, your determination, your persistence, your courage, your kindness to others, your belief in yourself, your appreciation and your gratefulness is what defines you not how much money or material wealth you may have, or what your current circumstances are.

A special mention to my friend and a beautiful woman in Cambodia: Seng BouAddheka who published her story of survival and renewal from the Killing Fields of Cambodia last year "If on Earth There are Angels".

Colleen Roberts is a Content Marketing Specialist from Perth, Australia

Inspiration 160

Hold True to Yourself

Linda Jabs

"To be yourself in a world that is constantly trying to make you something else is the greatest accomplishment."
– Ralph Waldo Emerson

There was a point in my young life where I had a number of life altering events happening in short succession and I found myself completely overwhelmed. The only way I could cope was to completely shut down and in doing that, I lost myself. It took me many years to find who I truly was once again and when I found myself and my voice, I vowed never to lose it again.

I would like to say that I have managed to keep myself intact since then and for the most part I have. Having said that, when I have had challenges, it has been a struggle to remain true to myself and have on occasion gone down a path where I have started to lose myself again. You may feel like that as well in your challenges with the journey known as life.

Stay true to yourself and no matter where the path takes you or what the path may be, it will be the right one because you are honoring yourself and accomplishing what is right for you. Trust in yourself and never let who you are go because that is the most important thing of all.

Linda Jabs is a Consultation Advisor
from Alberta, Canada

Do Less

Maria Paterakis

Are you a Superwoman? I don't know a woman who isn't. With today's pressures, are you doing the work of three Superwomen? What is the cost to your loved ones, your career and most importantly, to you? Is this generation of "empowered" women still walking in their mother's footstep? Sayings like "A woman's work is never done"; or "A woman can have it all" add pressure.

What does this all mean? For many women it's a rollercoaster. "Our work is never done" and "we don't feel like we have it all". Along the way the three times Superwoman feels like a failure, guilty, ashamed, unworthy, and is resentful.

Women everywhere, it's time to empower ourselves by doing less. Madelaine Albright was asked several years ago about a woman having it all. She said: "Women can really do everything, but not all at the same time. Our life comes in segments and we need to take advantage of that."

So stay present, set boundaries and enjoy and celebrate every step of the feminine journey. Being a woman is amazing. There are human gifts that are unique only to us. What are you doing to enjoy and celebrate the gifts in you? It's time.

Maria Paterakis is a Counsellor from Queensland, Australia

Inspiration 162

Cultivating Love

Shanti Clements

Sometimes love doesn't happen in the way we imagine. Sometimes we open our hearts and get hurt. Our hopes and dreams shattered unexpectedly. As we grow older, we come to realise that idealised love is illusory. Throw away the 'list' of the 'perfect partner'. Throw away conditions. True love comes from the soul and honours a deep, authentic connection between ourselves and others. Trust in your heart. Trust in your spirit. They will guide you.

I was 40 years old when I met my soulmate. My heart and spirit knew 'him' right away, just as he recognised me. We quickly discovered that we grew up in the same neighbourhood and that we'd gone to the same primary school. Why hadn't we found each other sooner? Because first we needed to learn to love ourselves before we could truly open our hearts to another.

Each day, reflect on the beauty within yourself and others. This is the starting point. Water the seeds of love, acceptance and openness daily through your thoughts, words and actions – whether it is for you, your soulmate, lover, sibling, parent, friend or work colleague. Love grows from love.

Be open to love. Cultivate love. It is well worth the wait. And it is well worth the journey.

Shanti Clements is a Principal, Leadership Coach and Writer from Sydney, Australia

You CAN Do Anything

Shari Ware

I used to weigh over 180kg. Everything was hard. It hurt to put my feet on the floor first thing in the morning. It hurt so much I cried. I didn't want to go anywhere or do anything. I felt ugly. I felt embarrassed for my family.

I put on a happy exterior, but inside I was a ball of misery. I had let fear drive me to that point. Fear of a relationship, because I had had a bad one and didn't want to repeat the experience.

Finally, one day I made the decision that enough was enough and I began the long, hard task of losing the weight. I lost 100kg and gained such an amazing life in the process. I wasn't sure in the beginning if I could come back from the dark place I had taken myself to for all those years, but one of the most important lessons I learned over the course of my 100kg weight loss journey, is that you CAN do anything you tell yourself you can, and I am living proof! So go on, tell yourself you CAN today, and see what amazing things you achieve!

Shari Ware is a Weightloss Mindset Mentor from Brisbane, Australia

Inspiration 164

Who is not good enough?

Iris Du

"What makes you stand out, makes you unique; What makes you different, makes you beautiful."
– Iris Du

Did you know that at least 1 in 5 Australian women currently suffers from depression and 4 out of every 5 have serious self-esteem issues? This statistic is not only to Australian women, most women around the world can relate to this. Have you ever felt you are not good or worthy enough? I get that.

Life wasn't easy when I migrated to Australia at age of 14 on my own. I always wanted to fit in because I didn't feel I was good enough. Especially in 2012, when my husband left me, I lost my Job, my grandma and my two dogs all in the same year. I was drowning in this "I am not good enough" toxin.

That was the turning point for me. That year I found the secret to self-esteem and self-discovery. You must discover your inner-self to transform into your beautiful self, both inside and out. Then you just have to unleash this unstoppable superwoman power of yours and you can achieve anything you want in life.

Be an unstoppable superwoman today. Love yourself and no more Procrastination. Because you are not just good enough, you are beautiful enough from both inside and outside.

Iris Du is a Transformation Coach and inside out beauty coach from Melbourne, Australia

Inspiration 165

In Her Eyes

Bec Campbell

Do you love her, I first must ask?
Do you love who she is NOW,
Or are you stuck in the past?
Do you look upon her face and be critical of the lines?
The worry and the fear, the hurt and the reminds?
Do you see all the floors all the wrongs all the fails?
Do you focus on mistakes, the aged hands and broken nails?
Do you mask the worry lines with painted lips and forged smile.

Do you ever stop and wonder, stop and ponder for a while?
Who the soul is trapped within
Behind the eyes and saddened grin
Beneath the hurt and beneath the pain,
There lays her story, from whence she came

In her eyes the truth be told
Of a woman forged from gold
The purest kind, the purest love
To withstand it all and to rise above.

To be the strength for all in need
The Samaritan of hope
The mare of steed

So do you love her I must ask?
Or is she forgotten in a distant past?
Go seek her out just start somewhere
Start in the mirror you'll find her there.

Bec Campbell is a Psychic Medium from Melbourne, Australia

Inspiration 166

For Me

This is my list of what I am choosing to do for myself over the next 30 days

Inspiration 167

Touched by Faith

Luciane Sperling

Faith is what will give you the strength to go beyond your previous believed ability, but to sustain you in your journey you need to trust! Your journey will feel lighter when your trust is primarily based on your humility that your path is also guided by a powerful force above your own head.

Success is inescapable when walking in faith, believing in yourself and having a vision in mind based on your big "why" of doing something connected with your heart's desire. When you believe in your higher power, which I call God, the gifts you will receive are strength, acceptance, new life, integrity and trust; you will never walk in fear again.

Take action to start to work on your faith and be committed to your decisions, remember that making a decision to take action, isn't yet taking action. Switch on your "Action" button and be prepared for your success because the learnings will come while "doing it"…don't wait until you "are ready" because no one is never ready…get started! This is YOUR life – get Possession of it! You have greatness within you!

"Now faith is confidence in what we hope for, an assurance about what we do not see." – Hebrews 11:1.

Luciane Sperling is an Author, Inspirational Speaker and Global Entrepreneur from Sydney, Australia

Inspiration 168

True Beauty is in You

Jackie Wilson

Know that true beauty lives within you. When you realise this fact you will be amazed at what you find! Quite often as a woman we get lost in negative beliefs we have created through our life experience, judging ourselves against women we see around us or in the media. That was me. As a teenager and young woman, I felt ugly, I had low self esteem and self belief, with a constant feeling I wasn't good enough.

Many girls, teens and women believe beauty is measured by how we look, constantly striving to make ourselves feel more beautiful, with make-up, hair, clothes, even surgery. Yet we are rarely taught to look within to see our true beauty.

Exercise: Who do you admire?

- Take a piece of paper
- Write 3 names of people you admire
- Write down what qualities you admire about those people

These people are your mirror. You cannot see a quality in someone else unless it lies inside you! Go on a journey discovering more of your true beauty. You are an amazing woman, so let the truth shine out from inside you! SHINE brightly beautiful one!

Jackie Wilson is an Emotional Wellbeing Specialist from Nottingham, United Kingdom

From Broke to Abundant

Tracey Hall

Being valued and being of value was something I didn't even know existed. From age nine I was learning how to cook and clean. I can't imagine making my children do this and, more, putting adult responsibilities on a child's shoulders. You know, though, I am grateful that it was me that had this childhood and not my siblings (yes, they did endure some of it, too, but not all, thankfully). Learning to cook at an early age was actually something I loved, and still love doing it – a silver lining to an otherwise bleak life.

At age eleven I was earning money by handing out pamphlets for a jewellery store and then I went on to babysitting/ironing for my mother's friends. I needed to find a job at fifteen during the holidays so that I could go on to years 11 and 12. My mother wasn't going to pay for it, so if I wanted to stay in school I had to get the money myself. I worked at Maccas full-time and it felt great. I saved the money to pay for my books and fees.

Tracey Hall is a Mentor and Author from Melbourne Australia

Inspiration 170

Flow

Monika Miller

I remember feeling invisible, unworthy, hopeless and insignificant. Reaching out was so hard to do. Fearful, empty, paralyzed. Drowning in my own negative self-image, such a state. It was only yesterday, I felt like you. You are my inspiration. Your tears are your inspiration to carry on.

Set the internal pause button. Next steps – need to feel. Try meditation, yoga, hypnosis, focus wheel. There are many more steps to help you heal and grow. I needed to let go of what others think. I needed to trust myself and the flow of life. I had to ask for help. I wrote this for you. I send you courage and healing. It is our neuropathways already paved that makes it painful. We need new ones ASAP. There are different ways to cope. You can carve new pathways now and have a life with more ease.

Breathe in, pause, listen, breathe out and release. Breath in, pause and listen to your heart beating, breathe out and release. Your heart and mind create your power through your soul. They have the ability to take you anywhere, be anything and do anything you dream of. No matter what, you can do it.

Believe.

Monika Miller is a Registered Reflexologist
and Children's Yoga Teacher
from Ottawa, Canada

Inspiration 171

Finding Grace in Grief

Sandra Wallin

The dark horse was waiting. The field was covered in deep snow and she was blanketed in white. Her eyes held an invitation. I walked forward, accepting. Head to head, a silent conversation began about endings and beginnings and how our essential nature emerges when the guarded casing of our heart dissolves.

I turned my face upward. Flakes landed upon my cheeks, then quickly melted into the tears that sprang from my eyes. Grace dropped her nose to my heart, breathing into it while silently articulating the essence of each loss, one after the other, going back beyond the chapter of this year.

With each consoling breath, I was shown that love can take a different form than the one originally made for it.

I noticed myself exhale… a deep sigh that carried with it a letting go and a letting in.

I've never thought about grief in term of stages, which infers that at some point there is a final stage, on the other side of which grieving is done. For me, it feels more like an ocean, with ebbs and flows, comings and goings, teaching my heart to be a graceful fulcrum, balancing the fleeting and the eternal …

Sandra Wallin is a Teacher and Psychotherapist from Maple Ridge, Canada

Inspiration 172

Simply Joy

Ruth Cyster-Stuettgen

Sometimes it is the simplest of acts that brings the greatest and purest joy. A heartfelt note written by a friend and fellow teacher, whom I got to share classrooms with at times, stays in my heart forever. A special gift through words, handwritten as a poem and decorated, I have kept since 2010!

> Dear Ruth,
> We've been thru stress and had a laugh
> We met as parents and worked as staff
> The friendship of our sons has grown
> given us the opportunity to be known
> I've loved having you at school
> Getting to know you has been really cool
> Thanks for your kindness, support and laughter
> Wishing you all the best for 2011 and ever after!
> love from Desirée – Dec 2010

How many treasured moments and acts can YOU gather in your hearts and minds, as giver and receiver?

Ruth Cyster-Stuettgen is an Author, Speaker, Coach from Melbourne, Australia

Turning Points

Louise Plant

I was 21, alone and living in Adelaide when I started waking up in the middle of the night and I could not feel any sensation in my right leg. I would get out of bed and sometimes fall over as I was not able to support my own bodyweight. An aunty had died from Multiple Sclerosis and a Grandmother had had numerous hip replacements, it had to be one of those.

I did not know where to go, I was new to Adelaide, no friends or family. I was very alone with fear and panic in my mind. I decided to search for answers at a Spiritual church. I did not find answers there, though I discovered Creative Visualisation. I started to visualise little men in my body and they would start healing me, every night and every morning.

I can still see them, vivid as what they were many years ago. After a month the lack of sensation in my body went. I later married and had three wonderful children. I was not going to be beaten by a label or a disease, I had a life to live.

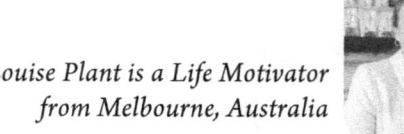

Louise Plant is a Life Motivator from Melbourne, Australia

Inspiration 174

Equality

Alma Ram

Traditionally, a girl child birth is, in the majority of cases, not rejoiced over. While the boy birth is celebrated. They say the girl needs more supervisory care, then gets married and becomes a member of another's home, therefore no benefit. We in the JBKS (Jagrati Bhalai Kendra Society) try to help change the mindset. We say both need the same.

Since this has gone on for more than a century, the birth rate is skewed. For every 1,000 live boys there are 900 girls born live. One hundred boys will not get married, so rape and sex crimes increase. Then due to taboos, girls are not meant to talk to boys. If she does, she is blamed. Around 2,000 girls are killed by (mainly) fathers every year. To marry, a dowry is asked (although illegal). Often she is beaten and even, after death, the family of the girl pays. If she outlives the husband (becomes a widow) they say she has 'eaten' him.

Why do I run this project? To change the mindset through small group discussion, males, mothers in law, mothers, and at puberty encourage games and painting, for both girls and boys, with teaching about equality. Helping the women to feel worthwhile. We can only take micro steps to develop the right thought.

Alma Ram runs a Maternal and Child Health Clinic Project in the Punjab, North India

Inspiration 175

Feminine Spirit Whisperings

Vicki Gotsis Ceraso

As you travel through your unique life-journey, thank your past for the lessons
Put your future on notice that you're ready to take your awe-inspired dreams with you
Choose to step into the life you crave to create but,
Do not forget to turn your dreams of today into the plans of tomorrow

When contemplating all the things you love and value
Please ensure to include yourself
For self-love is nourishment to your souls' stirring
And the forgiveness of your unavailing pursuit of approval

Do not take that which appears easy to you for granted
For these are your divine virtues disguised as gifts and talents
They were borne out of a longing to follow the luminous threads in the tapestry of your life
And deserve to be acknowledged and used in service to humanity

Understand, when you experience a breakdown
It will always follow with a breakthrough
When you stand face to face in front of an extraordinary challenge
Choose to see unexpected opportunities instead of imminent obstacles

Take time to breathe, to heal and become re-acquainted with yourself
Discover your voice, speak your truth and reclaim your life
Jump into your fears, set yourself free of all limitation and,
Create possibilities that have you giddy with unimaginable excitement and joy to be alive!

Vicki Gotsis Ceraso is a Kick Ass Life Strategist
from Melbourne, Australia

Inspiration 176

Break the Cycle

Kylie Farrugia

Your past does not have to control or shape your future. At the time I didn't fully understand just how powerful such a simple phrase, when acted upon with meaning, can make such a difference in one's life.

Unfortunately my childhood was not the greatest and I know that many others also have endured traumatic times. However "Tough Times Never Last, Tough People Do". The greatest gift we have as adults is being able to make the choice of saying "NO MORE" and letting the past go.

Out of adversity comes strength, courage and the power to overcome weakness. As a mother, wife and business owner, I am empowered that by being a positive role model I can "BREAK THE CYCLE". The power of one CAN make a difference.

Kylie Farrugia is a Community Worker and Personal Assistant from Melbourne, Australia

Inspiration 177

Self Worth

Zahia Araji

Growing up I had many doubts about myself, I thought my weight, lack of self-confidence and lack of self-worth would follow for the rest of my life and continue to be something I struggled with every day. It wasn't until I hit my mid-thirties that my perspective on myself began to change and from there my decade long journey to become the women I wanted to be began.

My first step was to break out of my comfort zone, my second step was to take risks and my third was to set and meet goals. By leaving my comfort zone and taking risks I could become a part of a company called Fifth Avenue Collection. Then by setting and meeting my goals I could turn a small risk into a career that would help me set larger goals and allow me to experience and be a part of things I only dreamed of when I was younger.

When I walk into a room today, I do it with confidence, I now know my self-worth and I now know that my dreams are not something that could be held back by the fear that I am not good enough.

*Zahia Araji is a Jewellery Stylist
from Melbourne, Australia*

Inspiration 178

Celebrate

*I am willing to celebrate the small and large wins.
Today I am celebrating ...*

Inspiration 179

Embrace the "NOW"

Nicole Maree Weatherley

Your Life is the Canvas, your thoughts are the paint. The movements you make are the brush strokes on the canvas called LIFE. It is entirely up to each individual artist what style of picture he paints. Each and every day he wakes a new Canvas awaits. - by Nicole Weatherley

Life is a sacred journey we are on, a "Spiritual" journey we are sharing with each other, in the beginning we are born, in the end we will all die something every one of us has in common. What we choose to do with the years in between is entirely our journey to plan, to live, to experience, to share with each other.

If you are yet to discover your spiritual nature maybe "now" is the time, I know for those of you reading this it is not by any accident it is by design, your life's design. On some level you have called this book to you so you can make choices about where you are "NOW" and where you want to be in a future "NOW" for that is ALL any of us have. Tomorrow's results will be a direct outcome of the designs and choices you are making and acting upon "NOW". As a young girl my grandmother had a tile above her pantry which read, "Yesterday is dead, forget it, tomorrow doesn't exist, don't worry. TODAY is here, so use IT".

My suggestion for you is to EMBRACE the "NOW" moment and use each day wisely and create your future "NOW" by design ...

Nicole Maree Weatherley is a Health and Wealth Mentor from Melbourne, Australia

Inspiration 180

It's About the 'Sparkle'

Chris Georgopoulos

Coal, when under pressure creates Diamonds! I came to be at a point in my life where I needed to find the appreciation for life as it was for me. Nearing 50 and having lived all my married life for my husband and my children, I had to find the courage to take a chance, to make a change so that my life would take on some meaning other than that of 'wife' or 'mother'. I craved to unleash my creativity and my inner self (my 'Gem') to the world. I felt I had wisdom to share and more than anything else, I desired new learning.

There was no place for me to go as I felt 'too old' for a career and not having mastered the technology of the day, too 'out of touch' for on-line learning. Thankfully I did not let that stop me and in 2010 I began my journey of creating an on-line business for women just like me who wanted more out of life.

Now in 2016, I can say that it's been the best time of my life and having a purpose is the ultimate fulfillment for anyone. We can all get stuck on how old or young we are, or how hard things are but if you don't take a chance, how will you know? Yes, it takes courage, time and focus to create your dream. All you need now are the tools so you can dig, deep down and unearth that Gem within and finally begin to 'Sparkle'.

Chris Georgopoulos is a Women's Mentor from Melbourne, Australia

Inspiration 181

Let the True Journey Begin

Anita Ferrari

'Do not look outside for the magnificence that is waiting to be discovered and owned within'

As a little girl I lived in a beautiful but quite isolated countryside. Later, however, rather than the distance it was people's busyness and 'I-focus' to hinder the deep connection I desired.

Years passed and even if my soul mate was by my side there was still loneliness in me: a loneliness that since the beginning did not spring from an external lack of connection or love, but from the inner, unrecognized beauty and value I failed to acknowledge and connect to.

The external loneliness had always been a gift in disguise, to help me turn inwards, open my eyes and find - as through the darkness in a cave - the marvels and riches within.

You are that hidden treasure! Recognizing your own beauty, power, value and connecting to who you really are hold the power to let your whole being bloom in the magnificent flower you are and create the extraordinary masterpiece that your life is meant to be.

Embrace yourself fully, completely, nonjudgmentally and the true path for you to walk on this Earth will reveal itself.

*Anita Ferrari is a Divine Healing Coach
from Sydney, Australia*

Inspiration 182

This Too Shall Pass

Karen Singery

This too shall pass is one of my favourite quotes and one that has been my motivation and support while going through immense change.

Nothing in life is ever constant. Life is continually evolving and moving. What happened a second ago has already passed. In a split second life can change for the better or worse. This change can either shatter you or make you leap for joy.

Ask yourself some really important and key questions that will help you to move through your challenging situation. Is this something that I have handled before? If your answer is "Yes" then ask yourself "What did I do that helped me through it?" Don't reinvent the wheel if you have done something and succeeded. Why not use it again? Should you answer "No" then ask yourself "What do I choose to do to handle the situation?

Life is a constant ebb and flow of beginnings and endings. Whatever you are going through will eventually come to an end. With every sunset, there is a sunrise. Love life, celebrate and make peace with change. Learn to dance with the movement of life. This too shall pass.

Karen Singery is an Occupation-Change Management Coach,
Speaker, Teacher and Teacher Aide
from Brisbane, Australia

Inspiration 183

Your Magical Life

Marion Hutton

Magic lies within you. Magic is the experience of manifestation – of all the prayers, hopes, wishes and dreams you communicate to the universe. The seat of manifestation lies with you. You have the power to create the life you desire through your thoughts, words and feelings and prayers. Whatever you communicate to the universe becomes your experience as is written in the Law of Attraction. You already have all the tools to manifest a wonderful life – the life you deserve.

First focus your thoughts upon what it is you desire. Then summon the energy in your body of how it would feel to be in this ideal state. Maintain this feeling until you intuitively know you are ready to release it to the universe. Once you do, send your request then let go of the outcome and allow the universe to deliver it to you in the most magical way with absolute Divine timing.

Create your magic today!

Marion Hutton is a Psychic and Intuitive Healer from Canberra, Australia

Inspiration 184

Everything Happens For a Reason

Sharon Anderson

Everyone has ups and downs, some more than others. People with mental health disorders can have mild or severe ups and downs. It is being talked about more, yet still has a long way to go. When someone is brave enough to ask for help, they should be able to get it. I learned the hard way that this isn't always the case. I was thankful to find a local resource centre to help me in my time of need.

They say everything happens for a reason. For me, a revised diagnosis has shed light on who I am and why I act the way I do. I now understand myself better and accept and love these things about me. It does not define me, it has made me who I am today for which I am grateful.

I am sharing my story to let you know if you are going through a hard time you are not alone, people care and love you. Mental health is nothing to be ashamed of, please ask for help and talk about how you are feeling to a professional.

Sharon Anderson is a Health and Transformation Coach from Ottawa, Canada

Inspiration 185

Embrace The Golden Muse in You

Chrisoula Sirigou

Dear Wild, Wise Muse, You are here to celebrate LIFE. You are here to help create alchemical transformations in people's hearts and minds. Let your inner Golden light shine your authentic, true, bright power. Embrace the qualities of the Muse in you as a goddess personifying knowledge, the arts, literature, music, rhythm and dance. On a quest to figure out who you are and how you can become more in alignment with your soul purpose, dig deep and mine for pure gold. Gold is the alchemy of its component parts, the pink and the yellow, colours of rebirth, renewal, re-creation and together they make up the gold of who you are now becoming.

You are called to be nothing less than the light you know yourself to be. Remember, with power comes responsibility. With this deeper connection and realisation of your golden self, you step up and say Yes to be of service, inspiring others like a Muse to embrace their own amazing light. The more you embrace the wisdom, the potential, the wealth of gold hidden inside, the more you embrace the amazing power to inspire and empower anyone who crosses your path effortlessly!

You are a Wild, Wise Muse and … You are Golden.

*Chrisoula Sirigou is a Colour Psychologist,
Teacher, Visionary Guide and Broadcaster from Crewe, England*

Connect with Your Heart

Fiona Craig

People struggle with what they want to be and do, and it's not because they aren't talented or capable, but because they didn't connect with their hearts desires. Visioning gives us the answers to those burning questions: what's my passion and purpose in life, and what's my true potential? Cultivating a vision requires heartfelt reflection and contemplation. Let's start with a simple Life Vision exercise. Imagine you're sitting in your favourite chair, looking back over your ideal life. Then ask yourself these questions:

The more specific you are in knowing what you want, the more you'll ignite your passions to work out your priorities and the choices to decide what you really want from life:

- Who are you as a person?
- What is it about you that people value?
- What qualities would you like more of in your life?
- What have you achieved?
- What are you proud of?
- What will you regret not having done?
- What legacy would you like to leave?

Fiona Craig is a Psychologist and Coach from Sydney, Australia

Inspiration 187

Dreams Do Come True

Lani Sharp

"Tell me, what is it you plan to do with your one wild and precious life?"
– Mary Oliver

I do not wish to know your name, the roles you play, how old you are, where you live, the stories of your past. Instead, I yearn to know what inspires you, moves you, shakes you, shifts you, makes your spirit come alive, and your soul dance. I want to ask you are you living the life you've imagined? Are you daring enough to believe? Do you awaken each day with profound faith, wonder, anticipation, and love in your heart? If you drew your last breath tomorrow, would you expire fulfilled, proud of your achievements and the mountains you moved? Do you live by your loftiest aspirations, your highest codes, your noblest desires, and the deepest breathings of your heart? Are you moving ever upwards and expanding in every direction?

If we cannot fathom the edges of the Universe and its number of galaxies, the magnitude of our minds, the power of our thoughts, the potential of our greatness, the infinitude of our visions, the depths of our souls, or the heights of our spirits, then how can we possibly fathom how big we can dream? For I only want to ask you two questions and they will tell me whole worlds about you: What is your dream? And my dear Child of the Universe, have you summoned the courage and the power to truly live it?

Lani Sharp is an Author, Astrologer, Healer, Lightworker and Eternal Student of Magic from Melbourne, Australia

Follow Your Purpose

Margaret Hiatt

"Dare to dream big dreams and follow them. Above all, believe in yourself, follow your heart, and have fun."

These are words I live by. Life is short and very often we forget this. We have one chance to live life to the fullest and to make a difference. If you have a burning desire, a dream, something inside you that you cannot explain, however you know it is something you really want to do or achieve, go for it. Don't let anyone take your dreams away from you.

Take whatever action you need to take to make it happen. Do it for yourself. Find your purpose. It is most likely the thing you love doing. Be bold and courageous. Do whatever it takes to overcome your fears.

Stand in your power and follow your passion. Allow the time and space for your dreams to come to fruition and let the magic happen.

If you have the desire and believe in yourself enough you will find the courage within you to achieve your dreams. Accept there will be challenges and knockbacks along the way. Keep going. Take massive action and never, ever, give up. Keep dreaming.

Margaret Hiatt is an Author, Speaker and Mentor from Melbourne, Australia

Inspiration 189

Create Your Future

Adele Haussmann

To be enthusiastic about the future YOU have to create it. You have to break through the fog that makes up your life, be disciplined in what you allow yourself to think, and take back control of your emotions. Suddenly you'll have hope, courage, and enthusiasm. Life becomes fun and each day an adventure. The feeling of dread is replaced with a high level of excitement!

Write down what you DO and DON'T like about your life. Work out a plan to turn the DON'TS into positives. What would you like to achieve? Identify your passions and strengths, work out what they could create, look at the skills required and make an ACTION plan to achieve them. Identify your weaknesses and work on strengthening them.

I wanted to create a business with happy positive energy for my family. It evolved into Smile Fitness! Illustrating you have to trust your gut and the universe and go with every open door.

As a parent take care of your physical and mental health. This will ensure you're happy. Be careful not to burn out, suddenly you'll wake up and realise that you've lost 20 years of your life!

…And remember, 'YOU'RE NEVER FULLY DRESSED WITHOUT A SMILE.'

Adele Haussmann is a Fitness, Beauty and Styling Professional from Canberra, Australia

The Joy of Style

Christine Maikousis

A woman's style says so much about who she is. It expresses to the world how she feels about herself and how she wants to be seen.

I am intrigued how so many women can go through life not caring or placing any attention to their everyday style. They find limiting beliefs about themselves that may or may not be true – which prevents them from dressing in a way that makes them feel unique, beautiful and even stylish. Beliefs, such as their AGE, their BODY SHAPE, their SIZE – even their BUDGET. But having great style has nothing to do with any of these.

If a woman wants to improve and elevate her style to look and feel great about herself then she must first work: WITH her age, WITH her body shape, and WITH her size, NOT against it!

She must know who she is, how she would like to be seen, where she is going in life and then dress for it. This is the key for having real style success.

Once discovered, a woman will then be rewarded with the joy of truly loving what she wears everyday; enjoying her wardrobe and looking and feeling great about her looks daily. Her size, shape and even her age no longer become an issue for her. Imagine how this could influence her life? How her confidence would soar? She may even become unstoppable ...

Christine Maikousis is a Personal Stylist from Melbourne, Australia

The Cycle of Inspiration

Christine Williams

Imagining ~ Nurturing ~ Success ~ Purpose ~ Integrated ~ Reflecting ~ Evolved

When I look back to the first dark days as a newly single mum, I never thought I'd be able to start again. After a rough childhood, I'd married young to escape, but here I was alone, starting again. My experiences of financial hardship went deep. I spent several years living in a caravan as it was all my parents could afford. I was determined my kids wouldn't know what it was like to struggle.

Things turned around the moment I developed a clear vision – a future where we were safe, loved and free. It was then I realised a very simple truth: *Imagining you can is the first action towards the level of inspiration needed when starting a journey of achievement.*

I soon learnt that nurturing my imagination created success, which in turn gave me the purpose to continually follow through with my goals. Each activity integrated my success into my everyday world. Now I motivate those around me by reflecting on my experiences: creating a cycle of inspiration that evolved from just one single seed of an idea.

Christine Williams is a Property Advisor from Melbourne, Australia

Inspiration 192

Never Too Late

Benetta Wainman

Never say never. It is often so easy to say that you can't rather than you can. It sometimes takes time to negotiate how you can, but with some extra thought and effort, whatever you really want can happen. Visualise it, really let your imagination take flight, know how that thing you desire looks, smells, tastes, sounds and feels.

You see I always wanted to be my own boss, so that I could see clients when and how I wanted. No restraints on time or purpose but it wasn't until I was 58 that this came about. It wasn't the best time to do so as my husband was out of work but I knew that if I didn't do it at that time that this time may never come again. I jumped, a little blindly, but it seemed like the right thing to do. Since that time I have become an author and plan to write another book early in 2017. I am still expanding my business but plan on another to help people to live with cancer in the most productive way possible.

Live every day like it's your last and never give up on your dreams!

Benetta Wainman is a Hypnotherapist from Melbourne, Australia

Gratitude, Parents and Forgiveness

Desiree Blaich

"Adopt an Attitude of Gratitude." (President Thomas S. Monson):

Gratitude changes your whole outlook and perspective on life. Adopting an "Attitude of Gratitude" and thanking God for blessings daily brings peace and happiness into our lives. "Count your blessings, name them one by one…"

"The most powerful teaching of children is by the example of their parents." (Dallin H. Oaks):

I am so grateful for wonderful parents, their fine example and unconditional love. They have sacrificed so much for me. During my triumphs and trials, they have always been there for me. I am who I am today because of them. "Honour thy mother and thy father."

Don't let others define who you are and forgive often.

I used to let the actions of others define who I was. I didn't like it so I decided to change. I prayed to God for his help. Gradually I realised that the only one who defines me is God. I am a child of God. I am precious in His eyes. I prayed for strength and I began to feel peace again.

Desiree Blaich is a Teacher from Melbourne, Australia

Inspiration 194

Step into Your Greatness Queen

Maxine Palmer-Hunter

Hey QUEEN. Life is full of a roller coaster of emotions that throws you up and down and leaves you filled with a frenzy of turmolic madness that never seems to cease. You want to give it up and give in to the feelings.

Right Queen! Stop right there. Breathe ... Look at yourself in the mirror. Come on you can do it ...

Let me remind you: WHO you are – An OVERCOMER. WHO are you? A VICTORIOUS LADY. WHO are you? A female of STRENGTH and RESILIENCE. WHO are you? A WOMAN OF SUBSTANCE.

Remember your GREATNESS. TODAY you may not feel ready to face the world, the burden on you is too great, the suffocation of life is zapping your energy, the people around you do not understand your pain. Challenges concerning family, work, studies, business, friends, partner or yourself are threatening your inner peace and you can't see how to carry on because of the weight of them on your weary mind and body.

YOU ARE ALIVE FOR A REASON. THERE IS NO MORE POWERFUL FORCE THAN A WOMAN DETERMINED TO RISE AND YOU ARE that female regardless of your age, your professional or personal stance in life, wherever your journey is at, no matter how large or small you have achieved. You ARE WORTHY. STEP INTO YOUR GREATNESS and be the STAR OF YOUR OWN STORY.

Maxine Palmer-Hunter is an Educator, Director, Author, Speaker and Mentor from Birmingham, England

Is Fear Holding You Back?

Rosemary Teed

My physical paralysis, caused by fear, was one of my greatest lessons. I'd just arrived in Fiji to attend a personal development course. Our first challenge was to climb a fifty foot pole harnessed, stand at the top and jump to catch a trapeze! My neck's capacity to 'go out' if jolted would be my opt-out; but I knew the real reason was my fear of heights. As people mastered the challenge, I found myself sharing idle conversation with a complete stranger.

Then I heard, "Rosemary, we will hoist you up – no need to climb." I was terrified as I asked Craig, my new friend, for help. I could hardly put one foot in front of the other walking to the harness area. My feet felt as if they were covered with cement and, without any warning, both my hands curled over like I'd been crippled with arthritis. Minutes later it was over. I'd even managed to let go of the safety rope.

Your fears, like mine, are nothing more than False Evidence Appearing Real.

Footnote: My story is dedicated to Craig who tragically passed away a few years later. I'll always remember his kindness when I asked for help.

Rosemary Teed is a Business Owner, Speaker, Author, Family Therapist from Melbourne, Australia

Inspiration 196

Touched by a Paw

Andrea Parascandalo

I lost track of all time. Thoughts were racing through my head so fast, one thing leading to another, but nothing made sense. I felt numb, so lost and totally consumed by the hurt.

The sun was going down and a striking sunset emerging on the horizon. It would have been truly breathtaking if I had allowed myself to see its beauty. But I was oblivious to everything and life felt utterly worthless. I was exhausted from crying all day, there were no tears left, just a massive void inside me.

The numbness was almost welcome after the shock and unbearable pain from losing my life partner. He was the one person I completely trusted and opened myself up to. Our love was unconditional and I thought our connection was forever. Something ever so soft brushed over my cheek and slowly my awareness of reality returned. Looking down, I saw the biggest bright green eyes looking up at me. Oscar was nudging me with his paw. I stroked him and he responded immediately, moving closer and settling on my chest rhythmically kneading me. His steady purr was mesmerising, so loud and the vibration so strong. The wave of contentment brought me comfort and I sensed the pure love and trust we shared.

I knew it was time to let go of the pain I was harbouring, so that I could move on. Life is not worthless, we have choices to make and dreams to live. The power of love can always be found in the smallest of places.

Andrea Parascandalo is a Business Manager from Melbourne, Australia

Inspiration 197

Random Act Of Kindness

Random acts of kindness I am planning over the next 30 days
(this can be something very simple that does not include money).
I am choosing to do what I can do more of and to support others.

Inspiration 198

Seize The Day

Bec Campbell

Who are you and where do you come from?
Emotions
Connections
What's right
What's wrong.

Wise beyond age
Beautiful beyond sight
A timeless soul in a transient life.

Mermaid to the seas
Angel to the sky
Pixie of the Fae
Yogi of the mind.

Keeper of the dreams
Guardian of the night
Walker of the shadows
Bearer of the Light

Behind the masks
Beyond the walls.

What do you see in the mirrors gaze?

The fairest of them all?
Time is fleeting
Moments pass
Nothing stays forever
Nothing lasts!

Find your truth
Search your soul
Reach for the stars
You can have it ALL!

You Past is a platform
One step in a timeless fate
Believe all things are possible
Carpe Diem
Seize the day.

Bec Campbell is a Psychic Medium from Melbourne, Australia

Inspiration 199

Winter Solstice

Emma Sidney

When Winter reaches the apex, we have the shortest day of the year and the longest night. This is a moment to pause, to nurture yourself and family and to give thanks for the lighter days to come. You may find yourself introverted, not feeling like doing much; in thought rather than in action. You may pause, like the seed under cold stony ground, planning to sprout but not quite ready yet.

To ground yourself, take a moment to reflect on the year that has passed. Write down your thoughts on how you have grown and changed. One way to keep in touch with the season is to walk at dawn (to gather energy) or at dusk (to relieve stress).

Another is to eat slow cooked meals, home made chicken soup and roasts. Don't forget to include garlic, onion, lemon and honey, all immune system boosters during colder months. Celebrations that we now recognise as Christmas traditions have always been common at the Winter Solstice, from the Roman Saturnalia, to the Scandanvian Juul, to Druidic traditions of holly and mistletoe.

So rejoice for this moment of pause. As the light grows, be thankful, celebrate and plan for the new dawn ahead. Winter Solstice – approx 20–22nd June (this is Summer in the Northern Hemisphere).

Emma Sidney is a Copywriter from Melbourne Australia

Inspiration 200

Some Advice

Levona Parker

What piece of advice would you give your 20-year old Self? As a young woman of 20, I had no chance to really think of my own life. I could not even think of marriage. At that time my parents expected that I worked to help the family financially. As a child in those days, you sort of tried to do your best.

It was not until I was over 30, that I could start thinking of myself. I would have loved to get married at 25 but instead it was at the age of 35 that I finally tied the knot. I offered up all those years for my parents. My advice to my 20 year old self would be to forget about what I don't have and make the best of what I do have in any given moment.

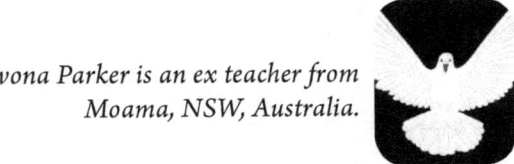

Levona Parker is an ex teacher from Moama, NSW, Australia.

Catharsis Through Writing

Jane Turner

I'd heard it said that, "It's never too late to have a happy childhood". But it wasn't until I was 52 that I found out that it was true. One of the wonderful and unexpected consequences of writing my story down for my first book *Thrive in Midlife*, is that it opened up a portal to an immense pool of love and connection with the mother that I never really managed to bond with before.

The backstory here is that I had learnt how to shut my feelings off when I was in the womb. I learnt this because that was what I needed to do to avoid being overwhelmed by the trauma involved in losing my twin in a case of Vanishing Twin Syndrome.

Despite my shut off feelings, I managed to have an incredibly cathartic experience when I wrote about being grateful that my daughter got to at least have a year with her grandmother before she passed away. I hadn't seen it coming at all, but even now I can feel the well of love that was opened up for me on that day.

I urge you to always feel your feelings, and to tap into the emotionally empowering activity of writing your story down if you ever suspect that there might be some healing of your inner child that's crying out to be done.

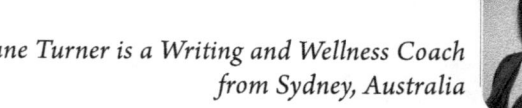

Jane Turner is a Writing and Wellness Coach from Sydney, Australia

Inspiration 202

You are Perfect

Margie O'Kane

My beautiful grand-daughter, as I look upon you sleeping peacefully, my mind wanders to your future life. I think how could I make your journey through this world easier. How I could tell you what I have learnt, what worked and what didn't. I could go on forever as only an older woman can, but you must heed your own council.

My one truth to you is that you are perfect in your imperfections. Celebrate all your differences; the way you look, think, and speak. Be proud of the fact that there is no one else like you. Be excited by what this uniqueness will do for you, what a remarkable, unduplicatable, and miraculous thing it is to be you. Of all the people who have come and gone on this earth, since the beginning of time not one of them is like you. You were meant to be different.

If you did not exist there would be a gap in the universe, something missing in the big plan. Treasure your uniqueness, it is a gift given only to you. It is given to you to enjoy and share with the world.

Always remember you are perfect in your imperfections.

Margie O'Kane is a Nurse, Midwife and Speaker from Melbourne, Australia

Our Cries Reach Out

Juliet Okoye

Our cries reach out. It was a cold Monday night close to midnight in mid January. It occurred to me how lonely I felt. I had been all alone after a separation for a few weeks. As soon as these emotions overwhelmed me I saw tears filling my eyes, I had been crying for long but did not notice.

Then I felt the presence of God at the end of my bed. It felt so real. I should be scared of this figure right at the end of my bed, but no, I felt comforted, at peace, all negative feelings disappeared all at once. The Lord had visited me!

Our loving father is so eager to show up when we need him the most. He is always close by, never far away. Our problem may not disappear immediately but the presence of the Almighty makes it bearable.

I do not know what you are going through today precious sister, seek the peace that only He can offer by seeking His face. His presence takes away feelings of fear, hopelessness, inadequacy, and loneliness.

His presence goes far beyond our imaginations. It does not only assure you that everything is going to be OK but it brings assurance, clarity and strength to fight and achieve. May your cry become a prayer that evokes His presence.

Juliet Okoye is a Continuing Health Assessor from Northampton, United Kingdom

Your Inner Truth

Josie Kearsey

What has a significant woman in your life told you, that has stuck with you for as long as you can remember? I would say many women have at various times all said that I have a generous heart and a spirit of giving and forgiving. That I have the ability to always see the bigger picture and many of them have made a point of saying 'never to change who I am'. Never to change my gentle approach to people and life.

That's who makes me Me. Right across my life, the women who I have hung around. That I have big heart and I just want to wrap everyone around in my arms. And those comments and encouragement I have taken on board and no matter the season, I always live by those words of wisdom and encouragement.

Other women speak into you, life, add into your life and are positive pillars for you to grow as a person. If the message about yourself is repeated over and over by women at various stages in your life, take heed, because they are a reflection of your own inner truth.

Josie Kearsey is an Event Director from Melbourne, Australia

All Answers Within

Brenda Dempsey

Feeling lost? Don't know which way to turn? Feeling overwhelmed by the fog which clouds your mind? It's time to evaporate the shadows of darkness you imprisoned yourself in; you wear the cloak of despair. You know enough is enough is enough! Your gut screams for something different. Lying naked no longer serves your need. You ask yourself, "What will I do? Who will I turn to? Who can help me?" "STOP!"

You are born to be free. Give yourself permission to remove the shackles of doubt, fear and guilt. Rise up like the phoenix, dance like the mystical dragonfly and soar like a bird on its wing. Live your liberated life.

You are a beautiful soul, limitless and born for a purpose. It's time for change. You need look no further than to yourself. Look inward. Glimpse that shard of light. Nourish it, cherish it and watch yourself flourish. Seek new ways of being. Meditate, for here you will learn to listen to your soul, quieten the gremlins and receive the wisdom from which you will grow, glow and flow in the abundance that is rightfully yours. All the answers you seek are within YOU!

Namaste!

Brenda Dempsey is an Energetic Coach from Surrey, England

Lifestyle in Your Golden Years

Elaine Squiers

What now? What Next? The greatest battles you'll have to face are within yourself. Every setback has within it the seeds of an equal or greater opportunity to change your life for the better.

Health and Happiness In The Golden Years is the Key to a very long life in retirement. The problem is that phrase describes the life we need to live if we want to feel good and look good. The health of your cells is crucial if you want to live a long, healthy and vibrant life. Why? Because cells provide the power for everything you do – from thinking to growing. Simply put, you cannot be healthy unless your cells are healthy. So, what does it actually mean?

A healthy person is described as a non-smoker, has a healthy weight, eats healthy foods and exercises on a regular basis. So simple yet so challenging to manage to do all of those things in our current world. The good news is you don't have to change everything at the same time. In fact, the trick to healthy living is making small changes each day, adding fruit to your cereal, having an extra glass of water or saying no to that second helping of buttery mashed potatoes.

So what else can you be doing to live healthily? Begin your exercising regime.

Elaine Squiers is an Author from Perth Australia

Your Story

Jacqui Hartley-Smith

"Once upon a time …" is an old-time traditional story beginning from long before today's fast-paced technological world.

Each of you has your very own, personal 'Once upon a time …' story and no matter what happens; no-one can ever take this away from you as it is …

   Unique – just like you
   Special – individually created for you
   Balanced – delicately and precisely; one of a kind, for you

Your colourful USB existence was being developed and stored in the Universe long before you were aware of it – from previous generations and lives – created to help you develop your values, your strengths and become aware of any weaknesses you may need to work on in this lifetime.

As your story unfolds there will be choices and opportunities to step out of your comfort zone; to find and explore what lights your fire within to ensure your life fulfils your deepest desires. Always remember that if your journey was continually comfortable, you would not learn and grow – so relish all parts of your USB story; learn to be kind to yourself, be grateful for what life brings and practise self-love to create the best 'Once upon a time …' you could have ever imagined.

*Jacqui Hartley-Smith is Self-employed
from Havelock North, New Zealand*

Inspiration 208

Tantric Approach to Menopause

Jenni Mears

Menopause can be a powerful initiation into the wisdom of being woman. I watched my own beautiful mother, who led a very purposeful and vital life, 'lose her juice' and disconnect from herself, then her relationship with my father. He stood by helplessly, doing the best he could with the little knowledge he had around the change of life, as my mother's vibrant health and well-being deteriorated.

At this reflective time in your life, you deserve to be cherished and celebrated. You deserve the joy of time, ease, flow, spaciousness, and aliveness. And an empowering toolkit full of guidance, embodied practices and knowledge, with the support of other women to navigate this sometimes challenging and magnificent mid-life journey home to you.

So claim your power as a wise woman. Be totally at home in your body, know your pathway to pleasure and be comfortable with your desires. You will be a force to be reckoned with. Invite menopause to be a time of expansion rather than contraction of your sexual energy. This can be a time to redefine what it means to be a positive sexual, wise and sensual woman living a vibrant and abundant life.

Jenni Mears is a Coach and Trainer from Melbourne, Australia

Do what Matters

Judy Mudie

"For I know the plans I have for you," says the Lord, "… plans for a hope and a future" Jeremiah 29:11
– The Bible

Hearing the words, 'You have Cancer' is devastating. Hearing the words, 'Your Cancer has returned' is soul shattering.

I was diagnosed with a rare Cancer in January 2015, given the "no evidence of disease" status in November 2015. By February 2016, the Cancer had returned. I was told that surgery could not remove it all. I would need chemotherapy for as long as there was a treatment available.

I had two choices, curl up in a corner or face it head on. Either way I still had to deal with having Cancer. I chose to get up and live the life I have been given. I still have bad days and sad days, but I am at peace, knowing God still has a plan for my life.

I do not know how many months or years I have left, but neither do you. No matter what you are facing you have two choices. Choose to get up and live the life you have been given, rest in God's peace and take the time to do what matters.

*Judy Mudie is a Retired Nurse Consultant
from Melbourne, Australia*

Inspiration 210

Inspiration

What has a significant woman in your life told YOU, that has stuck with you for as long as you can remember?

Finding My 'Big Sister'

Kimberley Bourgeois

I always wanted a 'Big Sister'. Someone to confide in, who would listen and laugh without judgement. SHE arrived ... as various people when I needed HER most.

When my 10 year marriage came to a tumbling end, I had no job, no income and no house. I did have my toy cockatoo, Cricket and friends. My friends showed up as the 'Big Sister' I longed for. SHE arrived through words of hope, hands that opened doors and love that provided a sense of belonging.

SHE came as 'Joyce'. She opened her home to Cricket and me and showed me inner strength in the midst of life's hurricane forces. SHE came as 'Emily'. She opened her home to Cricket, enabling me to launch a new career and rebuild my foundation. SHE came as 'Dalene'. She opened her arms to Cricket and me. We have never felt so safe, loved and wanted. SHE came as 'Brenda'. She showed me how to 'receive'. She brought me food, invited me away to clear my mind and connected me with people who required my services.

When my world seemingly crumbled, I found my 'Big Sister' in the rubble. With eyes wide open and heart broken open, she showed me that we all have a 'Big Sister' in us. I will share HER gifts with ALL Little Sisters on this life journey toward togetherness and wholeness.

'Big Sister' ... thank you for being you and being with me.

Kimberley Bourgeois is a Clarity Coach and Socialpreneur from Hammonds Plains, Canada

Inspiration 212

Take Risks

Jo Johnson

"Why not go out on a limb? That's where the fruit is."
– Mark Twain

Playing life 'safe' is one of the riskiest things you can do. It may sound counter-intuitive, but it's true. To create a life that's worth living, one that excites and fulfills you, that is worth writing about when you're 80, you must be prepared to do what is not expected of you.

One of the greatest times of my life was the period I spent backpacking around the world in my early twenties. I should have been starting my career but those years opened my eyes, taught me to love deeply, provided incredible heartache, released misconceptions, unleashed empathy, reinforced teachings, unlocked language, and created a new world view for me that no book or job could ever have. Some lessons were learnt the hard way and others in an incredibly fortunate twist of fate. Fundamentally I shaped the girl into the woman I am now.

Don't put off the experiences that may send you on a new trajectory because you're nervous about change. There's nothing surer than change in this world; I encourage you to embrace your own with outstretched arms and a smile. Travel the world, take risks, love fully, get your heart broken, create interesting stories and then go back for more.

Jo Johnson is a Content Coach and Author from Melbourne, Australia

Inspiration 213

The Rewards of Volunteering

Claire Sandell

I can't recommend enough the value of getting involved in a volunteering organisation. It enriches your life to be part of a community of like-minded people who are working towards the same goals. I have been a member of the Women's Service Club Soroptimist International for over a decade. It has given me wonderful friendships, taught me so much about the vast range of life experiences and brought me into contact with the many amazing projects undertaken locally and internationally that support women and girls.

The pace of modern life has become relentless. Ironically dedicating some of my precious time to volunteering and helping others brings fulfilling relief to the demands of balancing the many commitments of work and family. As an historian, I have examined women's stories across many different periods of time. It is clear that volunteering has always presented an opportunity for women to achieve and in turn help others. Much social change has been facilitated through volunteer programs in areas such as health, education and employment. At the turn of last century, under the veil of respectable Christian philanthropy, women were introducing factory girls to sex education, nutrition and further education. I am proud to be involved in the enduring tradition of volunteering.

Claire Sandell is an Historian and Business Owner from Melbourne, Australia

Inspiration 214

Letting Go

*Today I choose to let go of anything in my life that is holding me back.
Here is my list of five things I am choosing to let go during the next 30 days. So I will feel…*

Let it Happen

Isolde Martin

Inspiration, it is power, and it leads into innovation, or action into perhaps bigger and better things. In addition and ideally, it opens the door to personal satisfaction. So, let inspiration come to you! Ah, if it were not for cultural mores, understandings, and consensus that keep quite a few of us wavering and hesitating.

Have you heard of expressions like "she is just a naysayer", or, "this person is always opposition", or "one cannot really hold a discussion with her, she is just so opinionated". Many of us retreat under such criticism. Thus, we are taught to be agreeable, not demanding, not insisting, not standing up for ourselves too much in general. We must be good and easy to live with. It is clear though, that this hinders us to pursue our interests in full. Sometimes inspiration is taking a beating as it contains a challenge to throw off constrictions and follow and explore that vibe, that notion, that vague dawning of an idea. So let us become comfortable with our own notions. Let your inspiration take place despite our mores and critics, including our own inner critic. We must learn to say NO when it is called for, when we want to let that inspiration come in and see what it elicits in us. Be assertive!

Value your inspiration! Let your dreams meet it. You will be surprised what you can make happen. Inspiration can be lingering. But it can also be a moment's fleeting notion. It is up to you not to miss it.

Isolde Martin is a Psychologist from Mettenheim, Germany

Inspiration 216

Find Inner Silence

Clarissa Hughes

Find that deep quiet calm space that resides in each of us and use this to ground and support you through life's ups and downs.

In the "inner silence" you can put aside your over-active monkey mind, rest in the present moment, accepting everything just as it is and connect more deeply with yourself. And from that the sense of connection will develop greater compassion towards yourself and others.

So in your busy, noisy day try to carve out some time for silence, to reconnect, refresh and renew your sense of well-being. Whatever way you use to achieve that silence, be that meditation, walking or just being in nature, learn to cultivate it, embrace it, love it and know that silence truly is golden for your well-being.

Clarissa Hughes is a Mindfulness Teacher from Sydney, Australia

Fire Within Me

Nisha Ukani

Trust your intuition and the rest is created. I always thought life is a very simple, kind and positive gift of God. At the end of life, what really matters is what we built, what we shared, our character and significance. Live a life that matters, love and integrity. Be a woman who can heal herself and help to heal all the women before and after her with authenticity, vulnerability, transparency and moral courage.

As a woman I am so proud and grateful, until I realise it was a long journey where my inner critic was transferred to be my own inner cheerleader. Key to my thoughts seems a sense of individuality. I like to express anything which is awkward and imperfect because that's natural, that's real. Real soul has positive attitude towards life.

My Soul be full of self worth. I have always told myself that everyone in my life has something to teach me. There is a purpose. Purpose of being courageous and kind to help a struggling soul with an innocence of a child with no expectation.

This is me, adventurous means risking myself. Leave a little piece of Your thoughts behind in all those you meet along the beautiful journey of positive fire living within.

Nisha Ukani is an Artist, Jewellery Designer, Hairstylist from Melbourne Australia

Jumping Roadblocks

Elaine Squiers

Motivation Roadblocks And Recovery: "If only I were more motivated, I could get so much more done and be more successful?" Motivation seems so hard to find when we have to do something we've been dreading. Here are some questions and ideas to help you find it, keep it and overcome the most common roadblocks that might get in your way.

What is preventing you from following through on your efforts for a healthier life and make the necessary changes to live a Healthy Lifestyle? Is waning motivation preventing you from making the necessary changes to your diet? Is the thought of exercising too daunting? Maybe your illness or mobility issues (wheelchair, walking stick etc) make it all too hard. Are these your "reasons" for not doing any exercise at all? Consider what's standing in your way as it might be one of these roadblocks.

Is it Perfectionism? Are you so afraid of falling short of your goals or expectations that you don't even start the project? Do you worry that eating healthily and exercising will take hours of your time and leave you without results? This pressure prevents many people from attempting anything at all. They would rather not risk failure. My motto is nothing ventured nothing gained.

An extract from Elaine's, *A Healthy Lifestyle in Your Golden Years.*

Elaine Squiers is an Author from Perth, Australia

Who Am I Really?

Liesel Albrecht

A few years ago I had to relearn who I was, I had to peel away the layers and have that moment where everything became clear again. I had not been me for such a long time – I made a decision to go away with my two boys, then seven and 12 to Asia for three months, we left on my 40th birthday on our own Eat, Pray, Love adventure.

I was and still am a daughter, mother, sister, partner, ex-wife, cousin, niece and friend. But who was I? Who was I really? I didn't know, I was not sure I knew or even remembered who Liesel was, I had never just been me. I had to go away so I could begin the walk to my destiny. I knew what a good family looked like as I had grown up in one, I also knew what a violent relationship was as I had been in one. If I was to give you one piece of advice it would be to make sure you know who you are … that you have a deep connection with your soul so that you can walk the path you are here to walk.

Liesel Albrecht is The Retreat Specialist from Melbourne, Australia

Inspiration 220

Your Heart Longs To Sing!

Angi King

You came to this earth to have fun, to experience abundance and joy. You did not come here to learn hard lessons, to suffer, live in pain and scarcity. With your open mind, you eagerly listened and learnt and created so many beliefs, many which really do not serve you and block you from living a life you love and your true purpose.

Stop and listen to your heart, what is it saying to you? What is it calling you to do? Stop and notice what is happening around you, what does that little voice in your head say to you?

What you focus on, you see. Let's focus on what you want to achieve. It really is never too late. You can truly create a life you love! It just takes one step towards change and then another. Take small steps, really small steps. The key is in the momentum. Don't worry about how you will achieve it. Don't let that stop you from living your dreams. Just take the first step and look for the next. Your purpose is calling you and your heart longs to sing.

Angi King is a Presenter from Kingscliff, Australia

In the Name of Allah

Nida Mukhtar

Today despite the facilities of communication which should have brought people together, walls of hatred have been erected and hearts are being distanced from each other. Eventually when people get stressed, they tend to smoke, drink alcohol or take drugs. Whereas a solution given by the Holy Quran is: "It is in the remembrance of God that hearts can find comfort." [Al-Ra`d-13:29]. That is why, despite a thousand occupations, humans do not find their true well-being except in God. Having acquired great wealth or achieved high office their heart rebukes them all the time about their deep concern with the world and their conscience never approves their wiles and deceits and wrongful actions.

In today's world scant attention is being paid towards discharging the rights of others. So, we need to seriously think about how true peace can be established.

Hence for establishing peace, every person should sacrifice his/her own ego and discharge rights by acting fairly. We should cast our eye over our own life and should take pity upon our own condition by considering what we have made of our life. This will only happen when we recognize our Creator and only then will the rights of God's creation be discharged.

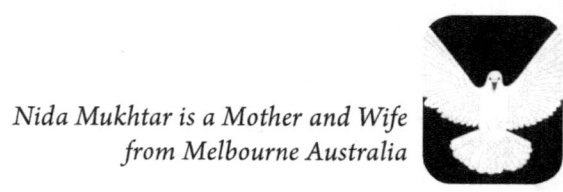

Nida Mukhtar is a Mother and Wife from Melbourne Australia

Inspiration 222

You Are Loved

Karen Hooper

I have to say I had a rocky start to life. Abuse, alcoholism, drugs and stress were entwined into the fabric of my life as a child as well as into my teenage years. I saw things and experienced things no child should. As a teenager and a young adult I had become destructive and I lived recklessly.

When I was twenty, someone told me there was a God who loved me "unconditionally". Some of you may have rolled your eyes at the mention of God but stay with me …

Never in my life had I understood or felt unconditional love. This was a game changer for me and it literally transformed my life from that time onward.

That hasn't meant my life has been a bed of roses or a continuous series of hallelujahs. I have suffered loss, failure, and disappointment at profound levels. My strength, and my go to have been that I am unconditionally loved, cherished and treasured. I am now a mother, which is such an amazing gift, a wife to a loving and fun man, a business owner and a relatively sane woman.

Know that you are unconditionally loved and treasured.

Karen Hooper is a Published author, Awarded Instructor, IBM Champion, Wife & Mother from Bayside, Melbourne, Australia

Inspiration 223

My Bucket List

List 20 things You intend to achieve in Your lifetime.

Inspiration 224

Purposeful Living

Alice Ntobedzi

"You are equipped with all you need to be a success. You may require guidance to clarify your vision and purpose."
– Alice Ntobedzi

Take time and sit quietly by yourself. Contemplate a vision and purpose for your life. What is it that you would like to bring to those around you and the world? What skills and talents do you possess? What are your personal values? The answers to these questions will reveal what is most important to you and will guide you to your source of inspiration, and the authentic you.

If you completely rely on the outside influences for validation, you lose touch with your essence.

When you understand yourself from the inside, you create your life from this place and access your inner power and potential. This way you also align your vision and purpose with who you are.

A purposeful life is that which is lived from the inside-out. You have in you, what you need to succeed. So believe in yourself!

Alice Ntobedzi is a Psychologist, Life Coach and Author from Botswana (living in Melbourne).

A Journey of Remembering

Beth Elaine Haynes

Complete magnificence is our ultimate Learning. The story that is our life is our journal of memories and experiences that make up our history, good, bad, indifferent, glorious and triumphant. It is our contribution to the evolution of mankind as we learn everyday that we can be all that we are, that we are GOD, that we are the example, that we are our greatest accomplished, the we are the consciousness that we are seeking. Gifting my clients one by one that they can contribute to the collective consciousness of humanity individually by embracing the totality of all that they are in this moment, in this moment of I AM.

In my 45 years of helping others find their calling, as my life's path has led me to mine. I recognised that what I was doing, was met with spontaneous results hence the birth of SPONTANEOUS RECOGNITION. What is your highest need NOW? With this recognition you are able to transition through the highest needs of your souls journey. So that you are able to live more consciously aligned to YOUR JOURNEY of REMEMBERING the totality of all that is you.

I AM.

Beth Elaine Haynes is an Energy Entrepreneur from Brisbane, Australia

Inspiration 226

Seeing the Hidden Blessings

Leah Jade

I feel it is a love of nature, life, humanity and learning that inspires great strength in a person. Tuning into the higher truth that nothing is truly black, white, good or bad is also one of the most powerful lessons I have learned. When we see that all hardships are hidden blessings, that all hurdles have great power to propel us forward and all setbacks give us deep determination to move forward, we are humbled by the balance that is universally always present.

To know that all hurt and pain can be transformed like compost for a garden, used to enrich our life, give us deeper roots and help us grow above and beyond, is in my eyes, the greatest asset we can possess. That inner wisdom is unshakable and empowering. When we have that clarity, nothing can get in our way. We become unstoppable on our mission to utilise and transform any challenge on the way, rather than letting it get "in our way". It is only then that we are truly able to use obstacles as our stepping stones to reach our highest potential for fulfilment in life. This wisdom gives us unwavering balance!

Leah Jade is an Author and Natural Therapist from Melbourne, Australia

It's About Perspective

Sharon Anderson

What advice would you give your younger self? If I could tell my younger self something that would help ease the challenges of life, I would say, it is all in your perspective. Everything will show up the way you think it will. If your inner dialogue is negative. Then negative is your outcome. If your inner voice is respectful, you will attract respect.

It is all in how you think, see and feel. Your destined blessed path is ready for you. You choose the degree of ease.

Sharon Anderson is a Health and Transformation Coach from Ottawa, Canada

Inspiration 228

Your Soul Mate

Andrea Maynard-Brade

A Soul Mate is someone that the Divine Creator of the universe has chosen for you, someone who compliments you, enhances your life, who completes you beautifully, someone who loves and adores you. Your deep relationship with God will enable you to recognise his voice connecting to your inner spirits and when you are both ready and whole your Soul Mate will be presented by the Divine Creator through Divine Confirmation to fulfil your purpose in life which has been ordained by the Creator.

Soul Mates don't connect through sex, looks, love at first sight or finances, you connect through the divine, spirit, love and light, so don't be distracted, your time here on earth is limited and precious.

To find your true Purpose in a Soul Mate, you need to wait on God's confirmation to make you whole, connect that Chemistry and Desire divinely. So firstly you need to find your true purpose before you get married, as choosing your own partner will be at your own detriment as it's not of God, it's of lust, passion, sexual attraction and sexual desire.

When you meet your true Soul Mate you should always be together (Married) 'What therefore God hath joined together let no man put asunder' Mark 10:9. True Soul Mates have Chemistry, Desire, Wholeness, Divine Confirmation, A sense of Purpose filled with Peace, Love and Light, so let the Divine Creator do his job and find your Soul Mate.

Andrea Maynard-Brade is a Master Health Coach
from Walsall, United Kingdom

Inspiration 229

Love What You Do

Sharon Anderson

In March 2014 at age 43 I had shooting pains down both arms, had a hard time finding the right words to say and tripped over things as I walked back to my office. I feared it was a stroke, yet didn't want to tell anyone. The following day I went to the ER and they found nothing wrong with me.

I went to see my family doctor and I can still hear the words as clear as can be. YOUR JOB IS GOING TO KILL YOU! Wow! I wasn't happy at work and knew I needed a break but this was a huge wake up call! The Doctor gave me eight weeks off due to burnout. Thank you Law of Attraction!

I took time to rest, work on my Law of Attraction coaching course and take The Passion Test to figure out what I was truly passionate about. As the saying goes "If you do what you love, you'll never work a day in your life".

Some things I've learned through this experience:

- Listen to what your body is communicating to you.
- Love what you do.
- Say "no" more often.
- Make time for yourself.
- You are not alone.

*Sharon Anderson is a Health and Transformation Coach
from Ottawa, Canada*

Inspiration 230

Let Me Love You Again

Bernie Giggins

Some secrets your Inner Child, your little self, wants to tell you: She's been left behind, held in spells or curses of old past beliefs and is waiting for you to return and release her. How you talk to her is also hurting her, she feels everything you say to her that is mean and nasty, please be kinder and more loving so she can reconnect with you and become one. She loves you so much when you are happy, laughing, having fun and is waiting for the day for more of this.

She says "I'm still in here waiting for you, no one else can help me but you, so by being quiet, closing your eyes and asking the magic question, "If this pain, sensation had a voice, what would it say to me?" Listen to the first thought that comes up, within five seconds, yes that's how fast I will answer. If you take longer, our controlling genie mind is interfering and keep me in this spell, curse and away from your heart.

Commit, believe in her and watch your world expand, I love you just the way you are.

Bernie Giggins is a Soul Journey Energy Coach from Queensland, Australia

Inspiration 231

Take Charge of Your Life

Dorcas Marimo

Did you know that only you is 100% responsible for your own life! Everyone has the power in them to shape their own destiny! But so many times we give the keys to our happiness or success to someone else and end up living a deflated life!

Life is a journey not a destination. And in that journey there will be trials and tribulations. How you react to them will be the result of the person you become.

Blaming your background, parents, that friend who betrayed you, that spouse who left you or anyone who has done you wrong will not change anything!

Just know you have some greatness in you to live the life you desire!

Dorcas Marimo is a Registered Nurse, Author and Business Woman. from Essex, United Kingdom

Inspiration 232

Invest in Yourself

Gaby Company

I am curious when was the last time that you invested in Yourself? Please don't misunderstand my question, I am not talking about buying expensive clothes, luxury cars, or investing in properties. Of course it is important to have investments for the future, there is no doubt of that. What I mean by that is investing in your Personal Growth as a Human being. If you want to be a Leader of your Life and not a follower you need to invest in Yourself.

Investing in Yourself will not only improve your Personal Life, it will improve the lives of People around you. Allocate time for Yourself exercising, reading, learning a course and spending quality time with your Family.

Many People complain about the lack of time they have available to read a book or exercise. However they don't realize how much time they are spending in front of the TV, games or social media.

They are two kinds of Human beings in Life. Those who put the effort to continue growing as a Human being to be Master of their own Life and the others who don't. They are just spectators of other people's achievements. They prefer to live under other people's shadows and accept what life dictates for them.

Gaby Company is a Success Mentor, Speaker, Author from Melbourne, Australia

Inspiration 233

Allowing Truth

Marie Ireland

Change equals Fear! We feel the fear of potentially losing something. But all we are losing is the part of ourselves we no longer require. We have known no other way, and every part of our being and emotions have been comfortable knowing exactly what to expect. This conditioning is what stops our growth. By letting our defenses down we allow our creative abilities to emerge and we begin to exceed our expectations which manifests unlimited possibilities. This is taking control of our life. If life is pushing you around it is because you are not taking responsibility for your emotions and actions. Look at your truth without the need to harm others by blaming, it is merely understanding your unconscious mind and seeing who you really are.

"The Level of Awareness will always validate a person's reasoning, therefore, the mind will Perceive what it is conditioned to Believe."
– Marie Ireland

Everything you act upon is lead by your subconscious. When your inner self is full of joy, focus, love and respect for yourself, you can then love others and create action to move forward in your journey to the life you really desire and deserve.

Marie Ireland is an Author and Business Owner from Queensland, Australia

The Biggest Regrets in life

Rosie Shalhoub

When St Peter greets me at the pearly gates of Heaven, sits me down with the big guy and asks "How did you live your life?" My reply - "With every breath inside of me"!

I started "Santa's Little Painter's" with only $5000 to my name. My friends thought it was just a hobby and my family told me not to do it. No way could I make money from a seasonal business. I didn't back down from their negative comments or reactions. Nicknamed "the lady with balls" I took the biggest risk of my life. Fast forward 20 years. Who would have thought personalising hand painted Christmas ornaments would generate in a short period of time a yearly income, with the added joy of bringing so much happiness to thousands upon thousands of people.

It was here my journey of self-discovery began. I realised without any risks in life, there could never be any room for achievement.

Listen to your heart, your own inner voice from within, to the nudging feeling you have when you just know there is something more you have to do with your life.

You won't let yourself down.

Rosie Shalhoub is a business owner, founder, CEO and star of her own reality TV show, from Sydney Australia

SUFFERING IN SILENCE SAFIYAH

Andrea Maynard-Brade

The 3 children and I spent the day at their Granma's, their father out looking about his business. Eight months pregnant with baby number 4, this unpleasant, throbbing pain would not go away.

My symptoms rapidly increased, I became weaker and weaker. Mr. R (children's father) was at a pub that night, leaving me with the 3 children at home. He came back periodically during the night to see if I was ok. I was afraid to lay down in bed, so I sat up straight with the pillows behind my head. I felt so alone, so I prayed, wondering how could someone be so heartless.

Early the next morning I felt my life drifting away from me. I called an ambulance which took me to the maternity, with symptoms of vomiting and diarrhoea. I gave birth that day to my still born daughter, she looked so beautiful. She looked alive, but there was no movement, no cries. I thought she would wake up but she didn't. They took her away and that was the last time I saw my Safiyah, the perfect one.

If I hadn't called the ambulance I would have ended up brain-damaged or dead, as the fluid was literally drained from my body.

Adapted extract from Andrea's work 'Suffering in Silence'.

Andrea Maynard-Brade is a Master Health Coach, Author, Speaker, Holistic Therapist and Director from Walsall, United Kingdom

Inspiration 236

SCHOOL

Khyrah Maynard-Ali

School is where your friends are,
School is where you behave
School can be fun
School is wearing my uniform
School is where you listen,
School is where you have to sit still,
School is where you keep your lips closed,
School is where you turn your brain on.
School is cool,
School is where you put your speaking voice on.

School is where you play
School is swimming club
School is where you sometimes fight.
School is nasty school dinners
School is where I bring my packed lunch
School is mummy dropping me off
School is reading, writing and maths.
School is drawing, drama and sports
What would I do without School?

Khyrah Maynard-Ali (age 7) is a student from Walsall, United Kingdom

Inspiration 237

Dedication

Colleen Roberts

"If on this Earth there are Angels."

This page is dedicated to Seng BouAddheka from Cambodia, whom I have personally met and worked with. Addheka and her story is very inspiring to me … The following is extracted from the back of her book *If on this Earth there are Angels*.

Addheka was a 14 year old Cambodian girl who had only just learned to walk after being a polio victim as an infant. She was part of the forced evacuation from Phnom Penh of the entire population of the city and trudged to an unknown future with her large extended family. For much of the next four years Addheka was alone, surviving unusual hardship and witnessing the irrational, murderous reality of the Khmer Rouge Regime. When it all ended, Addheka eventually returned to Phnom Penh to find out which of her family members had survived.

She remained in Cambodia and become part of the reconstruction effort, becoming a language teacher and Principal. She underwent a spiritual renewal and today runs the Aid Projects of Mercy which include establishing schools, the supply of basic school supplies and uniforms for at least 652 of the poorest children across 7 provinces in Cambodia. All proceeds from her book goes to these projects.

Colleen Roberts is a Content Marketing Specialist from Perth, Australia

Mental Muscle

Rita Joyan

"We must all suffer one of two things: the pain of discipline or the pain of regret."
– J Rohn.

My advice to myself and you, sweet reader, is a trait that keeps us upright and sought after, whether in study, the workforce or in business is our level of discipline. Some may refer to it as focus or commitment. They fall under the umbrella of discipline. Our ability to struggle against ourselves, to overcome laziness, to overcome the temptation to go the easy way, is our ultimate ticket to freedom, fulfillment and pleasure. Discipline takes a mighty amount of mental muscle. It's easy to let go, to follow the crowd. Even though we know we should, it's hard to keep to our word, to follow through on our commitments and keep focused on our individual God-given journey. It's too easy to lose focus and waste years comparing ourselves and feeling lost, whilst searching for that elusive something or someone.

Unlike the permanent pain of regret, enduring the pain and effort of becoming disciplined, provides freedom from wasting time, fulfillment of opportunities and the pleasure of arriving at the door of God with gratitude (not regret) for the time and opportunities in this gift of life.

Rita Joyan is a Business Owner and Entrepreneur from Canberra, Australia

To Do What It Takes

Terry Bahat

We all have aspirations to be healthier, fitter, stronger, lighter, more energetic and sexier. So, what are we prepared to do about it? There is a close link between the mind (your thinking, attitude, limiting beliefs, fears, desires, expectations) and the body. Our body is an adaptable organism, and even though the outside is capable of change, the inside (the psychological and the emotional) is a little slower to catch on. Mindset is the key to the process of changing your body.

No book, no diet, no personal trainer, no doctor, not even a dietician will get you fit. These are just resources. You are really the one getting yourself fit. You are the one doing the work and changing your behaviour, attitude and habits! You create your desired results. All you need is empowerment and inspiration to take complete control of your body, your future and your life, while you develop self-esteem, confidence and motivation for, finally, achieving a lasting, engaging personal transformation. I encourage you to question pre-existing beliefs, think outside your comfort zone and look at old issues from a fresh, new perspective.

So, love yourself; love your life as you are your greatest resource in every area of life. Remember: you can do, be, have and create everything you want. All you need is empowerment and the appropriate support along the way. You are the solution. I believe in you.

Terry Bahat is Your Resilience Coach and Fitness Partner from Melbourne, Australia

An A-Z Manifesto

Pina Cerminara

Here is a manifesto to inspire you to live your life with purpose, truth and joy. I hope this helps you to grow as a person, knowing that when times get tough you have the courage and principles to be who you love, do what you love and live your best life.

Acknowledge successes and celebrate. Breathe in courage and breathe out fear. Choose happiness. Don't give up. Embrace uncertainty and the unfamiliar. Focus on solutions and abundance. Give up perfection and take on progress. Have faith and trust your path. Invest in self-development. Jump at new opportunities. Keep life simple and fun. Listen to the warrior voice that says you can. Make a difference. Nurture and honour your mind and body. Offload what slows you down. Practice gratitude every day. Quickly forgive and let go. Radiate love to everyone every day. Smile often and laugh loudly. Take action to get results. Upgrade to the next version of you. Vibrate positive energy. Walk your talk. Xfactor your inner gift and give generously. Yearn for excellence and be extraordinary. Zoom into life's gifts and say thanks.

Pina Cerminara is a Business and Lifestyle Strategist from Melbourne, Australia

Pursuit of Happiness

Andrea Parascandalo

Life seems to be a myriad of experiences, reminiscent of the waves of the ocean. The exhilaration of riding the crest of a wave to fighting the undercurrent and the struggle from being dragged underwater. All we really seek is to float in serenity and bask in happiness.

There was a time when I thought finding unconditional love, trust and acceptance with another person would bring me happiness. Then I came to understand that ultimate happiness comes from within, not from another person. My heart was broken by the man I loved and trusted. A web of lies, mistrust, violence, and abuse, left me feeling rejected and worthless. I desperately hung on to our troubled relationship, existing in a world of hurt and gut wrenching pain that took me to the brink of suicide.

Relationships are complex and sometimes things change, the connection fades or loses purpose. Eventually one person needs the courage to end it. This is not rejection, just acknowledging that the relationship has run its course. Letting go seems so hard, but holding on to what once was, is destructive and so much more painful. You are such an amazing woman, with so much to offer and to be grateful for. Draw on your own strength and wisdom to let go of the past and accept the changes. Live in the now and focus on things that inspire your passion. You have the ability to find happiness from within and be at peace.

Andrea Parascandalo is a Business Manager
from Melbourne, Australia

Inspiration 242

Self Love

Loving myself first is what I choose.

Here is my list of what I can do to treat myself to more self-love.

Inspiration 243

Be The Inspiration

Yvette Lazare

If I am to inspire someone, I'd say 'love yourself first, seek God for His inspiration to match up to yours. Let it transform you so others can see God's inspiration of transformation.'

Starting with myself, how I have inspired myself throughout my life experiences, health, family and work - the bad and the good

Working with older people for nearly twenty years has helped reshape the way I live life.

It's made me think how life can change without any warning. You have to grow and learn how you handle LIFE, and how you treat others around you.

I suffered from painful joints and needed high level drugs to keep me relatively pain free. I could not work, sleep, nor lift my arms.

I was lucky to come out of it by going on a spiritual journey. I fed my mind with positive books and my body with healthy foods. I became more focussed and confident. I lost weight. I was hopeful again to have a better life.

Believe in yourself - spend time learning about you to find out what fruit you have stored within you. Use that fruit within you to sweeten someone's life.

Yvette Lazare lives in United Kingdom.

Inspiration 244

The Ripple Effect

Sarah Vitale

The Ripple Effect is about the ripple that a pebble makes when it is thrown across the water, like the pebble making ripples, we also create a ripple in people's lives every day.

Let me share a story. As I listened to a friend talk about her day, I could feel her stress and a general uneasiness about her. I respected the way she was feeling and I responded with calmness and a new perspective on her worries. I could see her shoulders drop as her perspective changed, she was heard and respected and realised that she wasn't alone in the way that she feels. Later that same week she called me and asked me out for a coffee. To my surprise when I got to the café there was a bunch of flowers waiting there for me. "What is this for?" I asked her. "This is for the effect that you had on me and my family the other day". She continued to tell me that the calming effect she felt was passed onto her partner and her kids when she returned home that day. She was more relaxed and therefore handled the worries she had at home with a new, calmer perspective and it rippled through to her family.

So, the interaction that we had was more powerful than either of us knew. The Ripple Effect …

Sarah Vitale is a Digital Marketer from Berwick, VIC Australia

Inspiration 245

Eat Healthy

Dai Shaya Maynard-Gayle

Sweets are not good, Sweets are not good. You need to Eat Healthy, you need to Eat Healthy. Don't make your sugar rush go over the top, put down those chocolate, pop and sweets right now.

I know they are really tasty, because I eat them as well, Sugar is bad for you and causes rotten teeth, Sugar makes you fat and gives you a wobbly belly, so children Eat Healthy, Eat Healthy.

I know you love the sweets as I do too, but fruits and veg are best for you, they keep you fit and strong. Sugar is bad for you and could make you die, so eat your fruit and veg daily as it may save your life, so Eat Healthy, Eat Healthy.

Eat Healthy

Dai Shaya Maynard-Gayle (age 8) is a student from Walsall, United Kingdom

Your Greatest Lesson

Emily Stuettgen

'What's the greatest lesson a woman should learn? That since day one, she's already had everything she needs within herself. It's the world that convinced her she did not.'
– Rupi Kaur

This is one of my favourite quotes from an incredibly talented writer, Rupi Kaur. Displayed on the wardrobe door, in my bedroom, it subtly supports me each day. I use it as a motivational factor, a reminder to love myself, and to remember that I have all I need within myself, and to always believe in my own abilities, to not give in to doubt, and to appreciate my own individuality. Acceptance and self love are possible to achieve, and a talent that is much appreciated through delicate practice.

Know that you have everything you need within you right now.

Emily Stuettgen is a Student from Melbourne, Australia

Inspiration 247

Shine Bright Like a Diamond

Rosie Shalhoub

Being a naturally inquisitive child I would find myself in situations and places where I was not only seen but heard as well.

It was the 80's, I rebelled against the norm. My role models were game changers of the time, Madonna, Boy George, "The Breakfast Club" tribe, the misfits, the rebels, the outspoken ones and the fishes out of water. I learnt you had to stand out, be seen and do it with every bit of confidence and oomph you had inside of you. Fast forward 30 years and I show my gratitude with a smile in my heart. I learnt it was OK to be different. It was in my favour to stand out. I created my own set of rules. Our era set the way for women around the world to explore their sexuality, accept their differences with conviction and passion.

I stand tall as I embrace every part of my womanhood with pride.

The woman inside me plays different roles daily from being a mother, wife, lover, sister, friend, business owner to a public figure.

I have learnt to enfold them all into one and I shine bright with every role I play.

Rosie Shalhoub is a business owner, founder, CEO and star of her own reality TV show, from Sydney Australia

Inspiration 248

I Focus On

ACHIEVING

Taking Care of You

Stephanie Wise

Too often we put everyone else first before ourselves, and we forget about the most important person. You have to take care of yourself in order to have the alignment and power to take care of others at the capacity that we do, as women. Do things that feel good for YOU, before anything else.

You are responsible for your own happiness. Do things that bring you joy, love and happiness. Carve time for adventure and have fun. Find a way to laugh daily. Nourish your body and mind. Always be learning and make a commitment to grow every day. Give yourself the best chance by giving yourself the best training, and always finish the race. Celebrate your wins, even if they are small. When you feel good, good can only follow. Make a promise to yourself to nurture yourself, love yourself and honour that. Everyone in your life will thank you!

Stephanie Wise is an Entrepreneur, Success Coach and Speaker from Ottawa, Canada

Inspiration 250

Paying it Forward

Stephanie Wise

There are people all around us who need inspiration. Reconnect with someone you haven't spoke to in a long time and tell them just how much they matter to you. Pay a compliment to someone. Complete a random act of kindness. You would be surprised at how those small things can shift someone's entire day. That's all it takes. If you are being the best you can be, in turn it will bring out the best in others.

If you are always growing, you gain wisdom and there is such power in passing that onto others. It's at your fingertips so allow your talent to be used and appreciated, and make a positive impact in someone else's life. That which is not utilized is eliminated. Realize the power of your message and use it brilliantly to empower others. The world is waiting for you to share your talents, what are you waiting for?

Stephanie Wise is an Entrepreneur, Success Coach and Speaker from Ottawa, Canada

Inspiration 251

I Focus On

TAKING ACTION

Inspiration 252

Travel

Travel is a way of re-energising and educating myself.
My list of places I am planning to travel to.

Inspiration 253

I Focus On

LOVE

Inspiration 254

A Lifelong Relationship

Renee Olson

As a philanthropist, and most importantly, mother and grandmother, I understand what it takes to raise a daughter with love, guidance and support. Not every child has an equal opportunity to have a nurturing family surround them and many grow up in single-parent urban homes, which can put a child at risk for negative influences of inner city life. When I became a "BIG" to my "LITTLE" Ryan in 2012, she was just eight years old and my role was to be a trusted friend and spend quality time with my sweet little girl. Fast forward to 2017, Ryan is now 12 years old, on her way to becoming a teenager.

I thought it would be so helpful for Ryan to have a mentor like me with parenting and life experience, but the truth is, I enjoy the rich rewards of our special relationship, thanks to Big Brothers Big Sisters of America. Little Ryan and I have a bond that is forever. Our relationship is a treasure, and I recommend "mentoring" to every woman. Reach outside of your own life and embrace the life of a young child in need. It will enrich your spirit and your heart will grow boundlessly.

Renee Olson is a Chief Leadership Officer from Addison, United States

Inspiration 255

Follow Your Dreams

Rosine Ghantous

Hello, I have a question for you. Have you ever wanted to do something in your life, but didn't because you thought it's not possible? Have you been told before, you won't make it, it's complicated, many have tried before and failed?

Well, I am here to persuade you that nothing is impossible, and you can make it by having a passion and love for what you want to do. To have support by peers and family who care, and even if they don't, you yourself can be your very own motivator. When you hear that voice within you saying, "I'd really love to become ... an artist, a designer, or whatever it is that you truly desire." You will work just as hard to accomplish your goal, despite the hardship. Nothing is easy in life, so it is about time you stop putting negative thoughts, fears, excuses or blaming others for your failures. Look into the mirror and say, "I am unique, I am put on this earth to accomplish something in my life, I will keep doing what I love, till I get to what I want, despite the amount of times I fall".

Rosine Ghantous is a Designer from Melbourne, Australia

Inspiration 256

Take Time Out

Laura Stuettgen

"When I'm tired, I rest. I say, 'I can't be a superwoman today'."
– Jada Pinkett Smith

This appeals to me, in particular because it reminds me that it is okay not to have everything together every day. That sometimes, I can take the day off and just be 'not on the top of the world'. I spend that time just hanging on the couch, watching movies or playing with my dog.

Make sure, you take some time out to rest as well, no matter how busy things are around you. Your body and your spirit needs time out, time out from the stresses of life. Time to rejuvenate, rest and gather energy.

Laura Stuettgen is a Recruitment Consultant from Melbourne, Australia

Inspiration 257

Rise to Your Strength

Samara Egglezos

When someone or something brings you down, use that negativity to help make you stronger. If someone makes a rude comment on your appearance, take that sentence, and use it to build your confidence. It might sound absolutely crazy, but it works. You do you. If you want to wear a onesie out in public, go ahead! No one is going to stop you. You don't have to show skin, or wear makeup to stand out. You are beautiful just the way you are. Don't let a stupid phrase break you down. Don't think for one second that this girl is better than you, because we are all different and unique in our own way.

I get it. It's hard to have resilience. I know from experience. When I was younger, every single stupid phrase that was said, got to my head, only because I let it. I was young and fragile then. I once got told that when someone is mean to you, it helps make them feel stronger because they had the power to make someone feel weak. After a little while, I started to gain my self confidence again. Look at me now. I'm a confident teenager. I don't let words like these get to my head.

Show everyone what your made of. Bounce right back with positive attitude. Because that's who you are, a positive, beautiful young girl, who doesn't let negativity get in her way.

Samara Egglezos is a Student
from Melbourne, Australia

Inspiration 258

You Are Made to Impact

Emily Farmer

It's not being untrained or unprepared for life that makes us fail, it's fear. Fear has the ability to manipulate and consume us if we let it, but if you are willing to lay everything down on the line and take a leap of faith to conquer your goals, nothing can hold you back, nothing can stop you from achieving greatness.

You are an individual, made to impact and inspire the lives you meet, you have a mission, be expectant to conquer, be ready to achieve, don't doubt yourself, you are equipped for this mission. You carry the solution to achieving your goals. Believe in your capabilities, rely on your strength. Don't be so fixated on the impossibilities that you forget your abilities.

Emily Farmer is a Student from Melbourne, Australia

Inspiration 259

Make Friends with Your Money

Yvonne Morrison

Close your eyes and picture being with your best friend. See the attentive look in their eyes as they listen to you speak. See how at ease you are with them. At one stage, you were strangers but over time you got to know each other.

Become best friends with your money so regardless of where you find yourself, at whatever stage of your life, YOU can decide how having (or not having) money will impact your life. If this seems daunting or impossible start as you would a new friendship. Getting to know yourself around money. Spend open honest time together.

Being best friends with money isn't about restrictions. It's about knowing how you spend money. Consider putting $5 aside each week toward a goal, which once reached, you spend guilt-free and with all the fun in the world. Comfortably take the time to gain the skills on how to direct your money. The choice REALLY is yours – it is YOUR money. Begin (and be the first if necessary) to have open brave conversations about money.

Someone once said to me, 'money is neither good nor bad – it can be your best friend – the choice is yours'.

Yvonne Morrison is a Creator and Coach from Lower Hutt, New Zealand

Inspiration 260

Use Your POWER

Robyn Nelson

As unimaginable as it may see there are many times in life when we allow others to stifle our power. We allow ourselves to feel powerless at the mercy of other people's opinions, words and actions. This isn't the way to a happy life. You have to embrace your power.

This does not give you license to be aggressive or forceful in life. These emotions are not linked to personal power. Personal power is a knowing within yourself. When you know you are good at something, when you know you have an ability, when you know that something's right for you, even though others might think it's wrong for you ... when you know you can achieve something, even though people tell you you can't ... When you are clear in your direction but others aren't quite there yet ...

IGNORE THE NAYSAYERS and USE YOUR POWER.

Tap into the ability within you to be who you were put here to be. The world needs you. You have a purpose. There's a reason for you being on this planet. Learn all you can during your time here and use your power to fulfil your destiny.

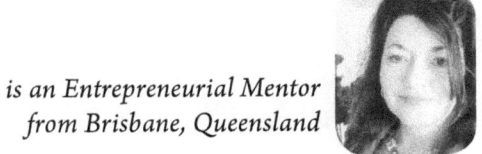

Robyn Nelson is an Entrepreneurial Mentor from Brisbane, Queensland

Inspiration 261

A Cat's Got Seven Lives

Rossana Fuentes

Sometimes when I look at cats, they remind me of life. Since childhood, Cats have been in the backyard. When they come into the kitchen, adults kicked them out. Not one of them have been fed or cared for properly. Sometimes I wondered if we, the humankind, are those unloved cats. I imagine seeing a dark cloud all over the planet but looking to the other side I see a hole. I push away with all my strength that fog into the hole until it disappears from my very eyes.

There have been many times when we have been STRONG and POWERLFUL, and have asserted our uniqueness and the right TO BE in this planet. The true self that resides within is STILL alive. There has been fog, though we have the tools to dig deep holes and let go of the unwanted energies in and around us.

The radiant and luminous self is ready and STRONGER than any foreign substance. There are many reasons why we can feed, nourish and care for ourselves. It is our LIGHT the one who need us. It's imperative, our light needs to shine = LET'S SHINE

Rossana Fuentes is an Emotional Life Supporter from Melbourne, Australia

Inspiration 262

Let the Breeze Caress You

Anita Ferrari

'The joy you have been seeking has been waiting for you within; are you willing to embrace it?'

There can be days when a subtle, sneaky feeling creeps in. Do not let that scare you my friend, nor hinder you from what you are meant and called to do. Let that be, let sadness, even despair or grief flow through you, so that they will find the way out along with old debris of former emotions, experiences and burdens still hiding within yourself.

Welcome that which you fear not to be able to bear, open your arms and embrace what has been waiting to be released, so that you will be the one to be set free. You will be the one to free yourself as you are the only one who can break the chains of sorrow, pain and regrets pulling you down.

Make your choice our friend, let that be one of joy, lightness and freedom. Let the morning breeze caress your whole being sweeping away the dust of the night and rekindle the fire of a brand new day, of an exciting, joyful life you have always been meant to live.

Anita Ferrari is a Divine Healing Coach, from Sydney, Australia

Inspiration 263

Love, Joy and Peace

Luisa Russo

"The joy you have been seeking has been waiting for you within; are you willing to embrace it?"

To weaken and expel fear within, the mind is to surrender to the heart. The heart works with the energy of the Universal Life Force. The hearts energy is natural, pure abundant and an expert at love. The heart does not find a need to try. The heart has carried inside it's core your Infinite Spirit.

Your Infinite Spirit's true nature is the pure essence of Love, Peace and Joy. The heart like a choir of angels sings and is patient and waits for the moment where your physical becomes aware of what makes your heart sing. Our soul knows why we have come to Earth and what it requires to Evolve. As our physical is a vessel for our Infinite Spirit, it is through our life experiences that our life purpose is revealed when we are open and ready. Life presents us with opportunities in every moment gifted to us; there is a chance to evolve.

We constantly evolve. To unlearn and release what no longer serves is the path to facing fears and healing self. When we heal we become limitless and in the flow of the magic of life. When we do what we love everyone feels it and we reclaim emotional freedom and Love, Joy and Peace flow from us without effort as this is our true nature. When we live in this vibration of our true nature, our Infinite Spirit experiences the miracle of the Great Spirit connecting us all.

Luisa Russo is a Spiritual Intuitive
from Melbourne, Australia

Inspiration 264

Affirmations

"I attract only peace into my life". This is my affirmation and I say this to myself each day. These are other affirmations I love ...

Inspiration 265

I Focus On

STRENGTH

Inspiration 266

Step into Your Power!

Ali-P

Sisters! Now is the time to step into our power! We have individually and collectively lived with feelings of shame, guilt, humiliation and powerlessness for too long now. It is time to move forward, look within and HEAL. The old patriarchal system is outdated and does not serve us, or the Earth. It is time to redress the imbalance of energies on the planet.

Let us rise up, bring forth and embody the Divine Feminine energies of love, support, compassion, understanding, nurturing and wisdom. As one woman heals her wounds, she heals those of our mothers, grandmothers, great grandmothers and beyond. This takes courage and is not always an easy path but the rewards are immense.

Let us not deny our feelings. Let us face them, FEEL them, breathe through them and let them go. Time to rise and break off the shackles. We are not victims. We are not powerless. We are powerFUL Goddesses! Light beings! Souls having a human experience.

Know that you are not alone! Call on God! Call on guides! Call on Angels! Call on Goddess energy! And always know that you are supported by the highest Divine source of TRUTH and LIGHT. And so it is.

*Ali-P is an Artist and DJ
from Lisburn, Northern Ireland*

Be Yourself, Uniquely You!

Maurissa Ailion

"If you are able to be yourself, then you have no competition. All you have to do is get closer and closer to that essence."
– Barbara Cook

To be you and experience a fulfilling life is not something that happens overnight. It is something that happens in fits and starts. Even the most self-assured women need self-knowledge, recognition of their strengths and values as a human being and noticing themselves in a positive way.

To succeed in our chosen life or vocation with dignity and authenticity requires energy, commitment and the capacity to flourish. To understand yourself and your identity and have a preparedness for the unknown challenges ahead. I believe you need to access your own individual life force, your strengths, values, and personal creativity.

Women are are always something to someone else. We hurdle through life as if it was an out-of-body experience, often loving everyone else on the planet too much and ourselves too little. Our world is what we make it, and living our true lives is how we add to it every day. I believe you need to recognise and value your own unique self and in doing so, you make it better and make a difference in the lives of others.

Maurissa Ailion is a Counsellor from Adelaide, Australia

Inspiration 268

You Are One

Pip Ransome

A cup of tea on the verandah on an early Autumn morning.

To the reader with love:

You are One with the Universe, the All. There is no separation. You are not alone, a single actor on a stage filled with unknown often threatening other. You are at home, here, now Held in the loving embrace of What Is. In this moment you are complete, whole, unblemished.

You are the sun's rays, scintillating perfect star-spread. The bee hovering at each delicious life-giving stamen. The mist rising lace-like from its nestling home amongst the earth. You are the endless pale, pale blue of the sky beyond. The wondrous, luscious crewcut of the gumleaves standing out against it. You are each petal each stamen of each individual four-star floret of each hydrangea flower. The shadows striping through the great floppy gingerplant leaves. The selfless pride, the flowing creamy strength of the eucalypt trunk. The tiny, perfectly complex ant climbing it. Oh! Open your heart! Let it burst asunder and reach out until you become All That You Are Merged, self-less into the limitless. Whole At last At Home.

Pip Ransome is a Dhamma (Buddhist meditation) teacher from Mornington Peninsula, Victoria, Australia

Mind and Movement

Illona J Shooter

"Who am I now?"

A question I had to ask myself after the death of my 20 year old daughter Jamilla. Jamilla had been terminally ill with renal failure for eight years and in that time I had become so much more than her mum. I was her nurse, physio, dialysis expert, best friend, and the giver of unconditional love. To cope I would put my runners on and walk where I'd do some serious mental preparation. The walking had more than just physical health benefits but mental as well, as I told myself, "You've got this, you can get through this, and you're strong". I did and I was!

Years later I am still asking myself 'that' question, but I am getting better at answering it. I continue to walk now that she has gone, but my self-talk has turned into something entirely different. I use it to reflect on the lessons she taught me and what I am grateful for. My Grateful Journal always begins with "I am grateful for Jamilla".

The mind is an incredibly powerful tool, which can help to heal you. So who am I now? I am Illona, I'm happy, healthy, loved and enough! :-)

Illona J Shooter is a Fashion Stylist from Melbourne, Australia

Inspiration 270

Choose the Way You Feel

Carolyn King

Life is full of adventures that we can choose to embark upon. There will be ups and downs. Sometimes these events are outside of our control. But what we do have control over is our thoughts and emotions. If you can choose to see these events through the eyes of an adventurer, life will flow more easily. Everything passes, nothing stays the same, including our emotional state. We have a choice. Live life with compassion, empathy, wonder and awe. Know that nothing stays the same and everything changes. Decide what your goals are and work towards them. Real, lasting happiness can take time, but when you find it, the simple joys in everyday living are amazing.

A few short years ago I was suffering from depression, feeling like the whole world was against me, and would be better off without me. Now I wake up every morning looking forward to the day ahead and cherishing every moment. You can too! Just know that how you feel today does not have to be how you feel tomorrow. Find what brings your joy and discover your own personal bliss!

Carolyn King is a Kinesiologist, Author, Speaker from Melbourne, Australia

You Are, You Can

Carla Trigo

There is nothing that can really break you again. The past is the stage where we put all the pieces to be able to build the most amazing life, is our core, our fire our inner power. In the past exist the magic of creation and resolution, is the opportunity and the POSSIBILITY OF LIGHT. YOU have a mission and your light is need it to embrace the Beauty in You ...

Down through the ages the ancient wisdom have been known: transmute the negative into positive, to breathe and connect to your power, cleansing rituals to lighten your soul and reconnect you to your divine wisdom, Be, Stay in your Authenticity, Walk your talk, create the YES.

No matter from where we came, what matters is the essence of your soul the one that is telling you Act, the one that is calling you to touch other souls. The shadows are just the opening door to heaven. Embrace light. EMBRACE YOURSELF, you are the reason AND THE WHY.

You are, you can, you will, you are beauty, you are goddess, you are joy, you came for a reason to fulfill your mission, to live your vision, to make a difference. You have important work to do.

YOU ARE ...

Carla Trigo is a Holistic Health and Life Coach from New York, USA

Inspiration 272

Happiness

I am happiest when I am ...

These are the things that make me feel happy and I choose to have more of these in my life each and every day.

Inspiration 273

Life – Don't Miss it!

Lyndie Jackson

"There are many things you think you can't do – until you do them!"
– Unknown

I almost missed the funnest and funniest day because of fear! I had been doing a five day course for public speaking. On day four I decided that I had learnt enough and didn't need to go back, as I couldn't find a topic for my speech. I usually like to finish what I start, so I talked myself into going, it was an hours drive away. I told myself that if there wasn't a carpark I could turn around and go home.

On the way, I noticed someone roll their ankle while they were crossing the road. They kept walking. There was a sign for me to keep going. Then, of course there was a carpark, so I knew I had to go in. I laughed so much, and had such fun. It was a really great day. That night, I realised if I had've listened to my fear, I would have missed the best day. It was then and there that I found my speech. So be aware of when you are resisting, it could be that you're on the verge of something really good!

Lyndie Jackson is a Remedial Massage Therapist, Reiki Master, Art of Feminine Presence Teacher from Melbourne, Australia

Inspiration 274

Spring Equinox

Emma Sidney

Equinox is an equal length day and night. We are about to soar into the long days and balmy nights of Summer and it's a great time to make plans to change and grow. During the Spring Equinox, we are reminded of balance and we can examine that in our lives as well. What do we want to achieve in the next few months? How can we maximise the light in our work, in our health and fitness?

This is also a moment to celebrate life and all around us the next generation of plants, animals and birds are being born, ready to grow and thrive. New seasonal vegetables and fruits are available, find them fresh and ripe, ditch slow cooked foods and move into salads. Think about freshening up your home, your fitness regime. In the Northern Hemisphere, this is the celebration to Ostara, many of the symbols of which we now associate with Easter. Fertility and new births symbolised by the egg and the bunny, also entertaining traditions where the men ran through the town and the women chose their celebratory mate for the evening. Have a 'Spring' in your step this Equinox and celebrate the coming of the light by taking a moment to dream BIG.

Spring (Vernal) Equinox approx. 20–22 September (this is Autumn in the Northern Hemisphere)

Emma Sidney is a Digital Copywriter from Melbourne, Australia

Three H's

Karen Hooper

To Honour; be Humble; have Humour. These words are very important to me, they frame my approach to life.

To Honour: We all have our strengths and we are all uniquely gifted. My desire is to honour people and appreciate them. I believe this is much more productive and gratifying than to compete with them.

Be Humble: Many of us have to achieve targets, reach deadlines, complete projects and that is just at our day jobs. We are mothers; wives and students. We battle with hormones, multi-tasking and having to keep it together. As woman we are all courageous, we just might not have recognized it in ourselves as yet.

Have Humour: Laughter relaxes the whole body; boosts the immune system; triggers the release of endorphins; protects the heart. Laughter protects our physical and emotional heart! To be able to laugh off a stressful situation, which potentially you have no control over, is the healthier option (and it will give you the nice laugh wrinkles instead of the ugly frown ones).

So today lets put some Cinderella magic in our day ... "Where there is kindness there is goodness. Where there is goodness there is magic!"

Karen Hooper is a Director, from Melbourne, Australia

Inspiration 276

You are ENOUGH

Shani Suttie

Where are you? Lost I see! Listen carefully. You have the right to feel what you feel, hear what you hear and see what you see. To want what you want ... Live according to your own truth so that you may be free.

Let go ... connect to all aspect of yourself –the beautiful YOU. Align yourself with what is within, what you know to be true. Live from your own heart space and see how that makes you feel.

Your feelings are guiding you ... Listen to what they say, they are real. Come back to the essence of who you truly are, empower yourself from deep within, by connecting you move back to your being, confident and comfortable in your own skin.

Remember we are all unique within ourselves and are here to play our part. Living your true essence. You are beautiful, powerful, funny and smart. You are here to live life fully, all experiences, to learn and grow.

One life ... no rehearsal ... take it, make it, remember you reap what you sow. Don't wait any longer, come into your own magnificance, make the start. Be guided by the intelligence within you, connect to your heart. You are ENOUGH.

Shani Suttie is a Breathwork Facilitator from Brisbane, Queensland

Inspiration 277

Stop, Pray and Listen

Brenda Saunders/Todd

"I stop and I pray and I listen…
I stop and I hear your every word…
I stop and I pray and I listen…
please show me a sign I've been heard.

My life has been a pleasure…
on this journey so far,
what more I have to offer…
is only from God's bar.

I've wondered and I've waited…
for many, many years…
I've even spent a lot of nights…
just drowning in my fears.

I'm open and I'm willing…
to be present and serve…
it's only with God's leadership…
I finally have the nerve.

I have a light that's bright and bold…
I know this deep within…
to keep it covered and locked up…
would be the greatest sin.

For God says each and every day…
is all there really is…
go out and give LOVE to the world…
and then you'll know you're His!

I'm really shocked and I'm in awe….
of this creative force…
from where it comes, I do not know…
I thank God as the Source!

From where it comes, I do not know…
I thank God as the Source!"

*Brenda Saunders/Todd is a Clarity Coach, Social
Entrepreneur and Executive Director
from Fall River, Canada*

Inspiration 278

You Are What You Think

Georgina Bajer

Dear beautiful Sister, You were created to love and be loved, to see life through the eyes of the creator, to be abundantly blessed and to live a fearless joyful life, joy that is only achieved a higher being, not the joy of the world. Your creator wants you, to seek him, in all your troubles and to good times, to be connected through the very essence of your soul. You are the daughter of a King, so don't accept the lies that you build up in your mind, words spoken by others, or negative words spoken by you, over you life...

Thoughts and words are very powerful, and shape your mind, you cannot control what thoughts enter your mind, but you have the power to control these thoughts, as your are a princess of the one and only creator, and he only wants the best for you, he gave you an amazing brain to help you think and enjoy life. He gave you choice, so choose to live life to the fullest, and to build your life, with healthy good thoughts, and positive words spoken.

" *Be careful how you think, your life is shaped by your thoughts.*" (*proverbs 4:23*).

Georgina Bajer is a Business Owner and Entrepreneur from Melbourne, Australia

Inspiration 279

No-one is Perfect

Ana Bogdanovska

Everyone suffers because they are not perfect. Everyone sees what is missing. Everyone sees the defect, the failures. Everyone sees what they don't have, but what if they stop wanting to be perfect? And if instead of seeing what is missing they see what is there?

What if, instead of seeing the bad, they see the good? And if instead of seeing what they don't have they see what they have? Well, no one is perfect, that's life.

Ana Bogdanovska is a Master of Laws LL.M. from Skopje, Republic of Macedonia

Inspiration 280

Manifest Your Abundant Life

Tanya Rogers

Manifesting has played a big part in getting me to where I am today. I began using the law of attraction in 2007 with results showing within two months. I began again consciously manifesting 10 months ago with over 1 million dollars debt, two properties that had not sold, and lack of purpose and direction in life. Within one week things turned around, I had a new life purpose and direction present itself to me, then within 24 weeks, both properties had sold and we had bought another one, cleared most debt, had unexpected income to the tune of almost $57000.00 come in. How I hear you ask? These are the few steps I follow to manifest changes in my life:

- Setting a specific and clear intent
- Visualisations and affirmations
- Goal setting
- Take action towards your goals
- Clear your blocks and let go of the outcome
- Have gratitude.

Following these steps will begin a creation process in your life, that is extremely powerful! We are always manifesting, but usually from a setting of default. We focus on all the negative things we don't want. By changing your focus to the positive things you want more of, a change will occur, no matter what! You can do it and you do deserve it too!

Tanya Rogers is a Registered Nurse, Grazier from Proston, Australia

Inspiration 281

Education

This is my list of the ways I am going to educate myself over the coming 12 months.

Am I Doing the Right Thing?

Leanne Woff

Proverbs 31: 15–18. 15: She gets up while it is still night; she provides food for her family and portions for her female servants. 16: She considers a field and buys it; out of her earnings she plants a vineyard. 17: She sets about her work vigorously; her arms are strong for her tasks. 18: She sees that her trading is profitable, and her lamp does not go out at night.

As mothers we are often conflicted about the balance between work and home. Should I work? Do I work too much? Do I not work enough? Are my children missing out? Am I doing the right thing? Much is said about the wives of the fifties who did not work at all. Was this good or was this bad? Well, the bible pre-dates this era quite significantly. What does it tell us? I love the verses in Proverbs that describe the perfect woman and guess what she works and she enjoys it and she is not scorned! I am not saying that to be a good woman you must work but rather I want to highlight that this woman does NOT feel guilty. She does as she sees fit to best support her family and does not look back. And for this she is uplifted.

These verses encourage me and I hope they will encourage you too!

Leanne Woff is a Virtual Assistant and Bookkeeper from Melbourne, Australia

Inspiration 283

Curiously Simple Inspiration

Toni-Maree Hannan

Inspiration exists in the simple, often mundane things of life. Like the glint of sunshine on a gum leaf, the lopsided grin of a full moons face, or the giggles of a baby as they see something like a butterfly for the very first time. These are reminders to live fully and purposefully. Paying attention to these seemingly mundane things allows us to live in the now and to forget our troubles, worries, disputes and disagreements.

Right now, take a curious look at the world around you and immerse yourself in your current location. Allow yourself to be absorbed by the sounds, emotions, sights and sensations around you. Let go of anything that disturbs or interferes with your concentration. Instead, discover the quiet joy and delight in focusing on your secret moment in time.

As you give yourself permission to focus, remember to breathe slowly and evenly. This moment is your gift to yourself. Full of possibility. Full of joy, wonder, peace and promise. In this moment, everything is achievable. It all comes effortlessly and easily.

Notice how calm and centred you feel. It's magical. Available at a moment's notice. This quiet space is where inspiration resides and you have it within you always. All you need to do is notice it.

Toni-Maree Hannan is a Life Coach from Canberra, Australia

Moments

Pauline M. Rohdich

"Life is not measured by the number of breaths we take, but by the moments that take our breath away."
– Maya Angelou

Live every moment with awareness. Know that each moment is new, fresh and never before experienced. Spend your moments creating memories with those you love. Cherish your family. Look for things that bring you joy. Choose your friends wisely, for it is a wise adage, " Show me your company and I'll tell you who you are."

Learn to love your body and every part of you. Look in the mirror and tell yourself you are beautiful, for self-love is the best romance of all. Commit to personal growth, ask questions and make sure you get the answers. The greatest study is the exploration of your self.

Don't let anyone steal your dreams, they are yours and yours alone to decipher and realize. Enjoy your own company, silent intervals and time for reflection. Don't waste your precious moments on trivia, bring meaning to everything you do and live from your highest vibration.

Laugh often and be the inspiration you seek from others. Commit to being the best YOU and create breath-taking moments forever.

Pauline M. Rohdich is a Life Coach, Speaker, Author and Web TV Host from Brisbane, Australia

Professional Bullying

Gameeda Henry

We were five sisters born into a family of nine. All of us have been subject to Professional Bullying at some time in our working lives. Whether it was through jealousy, rivalry, prejudice, racism, illness or stress, we have been treated as doormats after years of loyal service.

Teaching Accounts for more than 34 years, I was declared redundant by the Western Cape Education Department. Lifelong colleagues became prejudiced and backbiting became rife.

So yes ladies, you can be pushed and shoved, but if you do not surround yourself with positive, loveable people, you'll find yourself in a warzone and at the mercy of bullies.

Gameeda Henry is a Teacher from Stellenbosch, South Africa

Inspiration 286

You are Destined to Succeed

Christy Amalu

"What is one piece of advice you would give to your younger self?"

Be focused in life, work harder, grab every opportunity because they may never come your way again.

Christy Amalu is a Clinical Nurse Advisor from Milton Keynes UK

Leap of Faith

Annie Toscher

Overcoming perceived limitations I learned at the grand age of 12 years old. After having rheumatic fever at six years old that left me with a heart murmur, the doctors and my mum told me that I could not participate in any school sport or physical activity. So I became the kid who sat on the sideline cheering on all the others kids. In my heart I deeply yearned to run in an athletic race.

When my father suddenly uprooted my sisters and I from Wollongong to live in Warner's Bay it was frightening. Starting a new primary school I soon realized this was a golden opportunity to re-invent myself. It was a time of survival and being accountable to myself.

The school athletics carnival I entered my first age race. Having always been the kid who was not allowed to run I chose to go for it! I won that race and continued on throughout school to compete. That defining moment I've carried throughout my life especially when I have fear and doubt.

When we overcome our limitations and take that leap of faith we discover what we're really made of and surprise ourselves.

Annie Toscher is a Matrix Therapist, Passion and Purpose Coach, Co-Author "You Can Be Your Own Stylists" from Melbourne, Australia

Inspiration 288

I Focus On

SUPPORT

Inspiration 289

Be of Service, Not Sacrifice

Helen Bolger-Harris

I come from a long line of women in service, particularly teaching and nursing. I was a nurse and now I'm a coach and trainer and I'm regularly involved in volunteer work. However, whilst this is very noble, I allowed it to rob me of being of service to myself: I often sacrificed myself for others because I thought I was being selfless and being self-focused was selfish. Now I realise that being selfless means I'm 'less than myself' and being 'self-centred' isn't being selfish: it's centring myself first so then I can be of service to others.

This doesn't mean that we can't give to and share with others. But like our oxygen mask needs to be placed on ourselves first before others during a flight, even our own children, we must fill our own cup first and foremost.

Women tend to be nurturers by nature but sacrificing ourselves has become a habit for too many women. The results can include low self-esteem, stress, depression, anxiety and a lower quality of life. We can't truly acknowledge the beauty and divinity in others if we can't do so with ourselves first.

What self-nurturing are you serving yourself with today?

Helen Bolger-Harris is a Coach, Speaker, Trainer from Melbourne, Australia

Inspiration 290

Inspiration

I am inspired to ...

Resilience

Margaret Hiatt

There are countless stories of resilience and most are intertwined with stories of success. Very often we listen to these stories and believe this only happens to others.

Most of us have had situations in life that tested our resolve and then we've gone on to overcome the pain and the setbacks. It is what we learn from these setbacks, tragedies or failures; I believe, is the important part. When you are willing to take the time to learn and understand more about yourself because of the situations you've endured and how you tapped into your resilience, you'll move on more easily instead of continually living in the past and what I call Groundhog Day.

Oprah is a wonderful example of a woman who has overcome unthinkable situations to become the person she is today who shares her stories and those of others to make an impact in the world and change lives.

You too have a story. You have resilience. Choose to acknowledge your resilience and be aware of how you can turn negatives into positives by learning about yourself and by sharing with others so they also can make changes in their lives and those of others. .

Margaret Hiatt is an Author, Speaker and Mentor from Melbourne, Australia

Unleashing Your Inner Child

Brenda Dempsey

You are born to live a fulfilling life of joy, peace and abundance. You run freely, laugh loudly and explore like there is no tomorrow! Mistakes are not in your vocabulary only efforts that demonstrate courage, persistence and fearlessness. YOU learn all of the time from others, your environment and by assimilating everything around you to your world. You bring joy to everyone.

Then one day…all of that is taken from you. You become socialised to cultural norms, social expectations and a desire to please those you love. This diminishes who you truly are and the rules in which you become entrenched, suck the joy, awe and wonder out of you. An uninspiring education system expects you to behave in the same way but you are not the same; you are unique. You develop all sorts of insecurities and behaviours, for you kick against what your spirit truly longs for … freedom to do what you are meant to do; live a purposeful life full of love and joy.

All is not lost. You have temporarily buried yourself, like a pressured diamond; a time comes when you long for those peaceful exciting feelings of childhood. You emerge to unleash, once again, your diamond inner child.

Brenda Dempsey is an Energetic Coach from Surrey, England

Inspiration 293

I Love Being 80!

Ethelwynne Petersen

I now find myself a member of 'The Elite Eighties' – that's what we are, elite. My dictionary says 'elite' means the best, crème de la crème, the choice part of a larger group. Isn't that wonderful?

I love being 80! So, Friends, don't be afraid of growing old. My prayer each day to our heavenly Father is: 'help me to grow old graciously, to be more tolerant and understanding of our younger folk, or accepting of the Lord's will in my life and more thankful for those who understand my forgetfulness. And when I spill my tea or don't always eat all my food, or make unexpected mistakes.'

Life is a Gift from God, all tied up with a red ribbon and a big red bow. Go on enjoying your gift of life – loving one another, enjoying family and friendship, being a peacemaker and spreading a message of hope each day to your loved ones and those you meet each day.

Ethelwynne Petersen is Retired from Cape Town, South Africa

Inspiration 294

I Focus On

WORTHINESS

A Well Woman – Getting it Right

Christy Amalu

With today's busy lifestyles, finding time to visit the doctor can often be difficult but it is important not to forget about our health. Health checks do not take long and they do not need to be expensive. However, they have proved to be highly effective and in many cases early screening has literally saved lives. His spoken words that you hear and keep are spirit and impart the life of God to you.

Also, emotional wellness is having a positive attitude, high self-esteem, a strong sense of self and the ability to recognize and share a wide range of feelings with others in a constructive way. A tree that bears good fruits should be nurtured. "Make a tree good and its fruit will be good, or make a tree bad and its fruit will be bad, for a tree is recognized by its fruit."– Matt 12:33. This book elaborates what it takes to maintain optimum wellness both clinically, emotionally, spiritually, evangelically etc. A woman needs to be well in order to nurture others as the popular adage says to train a woman is to train a nation.

Extract from Christy Amalu's Book, *A Well Woman – Getting it Right*.

Christy Amalu is a Clinical Nurse Advisor from Milton Keynes, United Kingdom

Inspiration 296

It's Always the Darkest Before Dawn

Natalie Petersen

I know it sounds really cliché, but it's true – it's always darkest just before a new dawn. I had a job I loved. I was a teacher in a local primary school. I was good at it, I worked hard and the children in my care thrived. Then a group of colleagues started making things difficult for me. I never thought of it as bullying, they were quite subtle about it, but within six months I had a nervous breakdown and simply couldn't go to work. I felt embarrassed and ashamed that I wasn't coping. I felt confused and angry at my colleagues.

Eventually I took a voluntary departure package and walked away. We bought a camper trailer and took the family on a three month trip to North and Western Australia.

I had done a small business course. I gathered a bank of teachers to work for me as replacement teachers if someone was away. By the time I sold the business I was employing 250 teachers each year, had turned over 26 million dollars and had won an Australian Achiever Award with a customer service rating of 99.68%. I guess the moral of my story is this: In every job you do, you develop skills that can be transferred and built upon in your next, better job. Everything you are doing now is preparing you for your next, better job. The colleagues that gave me such a hard time actually come into my educational supply shop that I have now. When I see them, I just quietly thank them, because they helped me get to my next, better job.

Natalie Petersen is an Owner of a Book Store from Melbourne, Australia

Inspiration 297

It's All About You

Ali Greer

Young and simple, open and clear
Troubled but why?
Indifference in pain, with sadness
We try
Trauma, shock and confusion with loss
Nightmares of death
Hearses and all
We'll keep going that's for sure
Troublesome years the soul will bare
Many a time we'll shed our tears
With blankets of quiet we all live on
Anger and pain we feel full on
Never the less we stumble through
To adulthood we must be strong
We make our choices we make our way
With our life herstory
Leading the way
With our masks and personas we get through
But pain and sadness must subdue
Come the day we are all grown

And holding one of our own
Young and simple open and clear
But as they grow, live and learn
We look inside and have our turn
Tired of sadness, anger and pain
We'll begin our journey
We'll begin today.
Goodbye life herstory, it's my turn now
Welcome to all that makes you sound
Surround yourself with soulful beauty
Love yourself throughout this journey
It's all about you, so make it so
With love and light you will grow

Ali Greer produces hand drawn artwork
from Melbourne, Australia

A Celebration

Joanne Worthy

Celebrate the Woman that you have become. Dear Beautiful Woman, I know you have struggled, and you have experienced enormous trauma. I even know that as a little girl you were very insecure and you thought no one liked you. You had no confidence and very little self-love. You often felt alone and you were scared of everything and you felt like you never really fitted in. You would escape into a make believe world of fairytales to dull the inner torment. You were often bullied at school, and you felt like you did not have a voice; no-one really heard you. You felt ugly and worthless so people often treated you badly.

Now you stand in front of the mirror, you are now a wise magnificent woman. You are a woman who is imperfectly perfect. You are strong and courageous and you are not afraid to speak your truth. You have fought hard to become the woman you are today. You love and honour yourself deeply and are comfortable with who you are and what you stand for – you love your "inner child" and you have become love worthy.

Do you know the reason I know all this? I am also that woman.

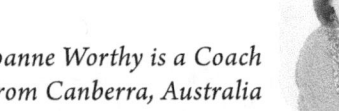

Joanne Worthy is a Coach from Canberra, Australia

Inspiration 299

What makes a Mummy Like Me ...

Linda Reed-Enever

A Mummy like me has taken 1,000 steps in many directions to get where she is.
She is not lucky she works hard,
She is human, wrinkled and flawed. All of what makes her the woman you love.
She is Mummy, wife and daughter as well as business woman and thought leader.
Her family means everything to her and she is the lioness that protects them.
She dared to dream and chased those dreams,
She has fallen more times than a child, but gets back up again.
She is creating a future, a path and a community for her children,
She is Mum, Mummy and Me doing the best she can, to be the best she can be.

*Linda Reed-Enever is an Entrepreneur
from Melbourne, Australia*

Inspiration 300

Yes, You Can

Grace Vassallo

My message is simple after living a life filled with insecurity, embarrassment, shyness and self-doubt. Do what you are passionate about and what your heart yearns more of. Acknowledge that fears, self-doubt and insecurities will come up and keep coming up. It's part of our survival mechanism as human beings. Fears served us when we were in the cave-man era, but in today's world, it hardly serves us. Life is for living. When you give in to fear and self-doubt, you forego the pleasures of living and living the most incredible, pinch-me life.

Recognise what is an emotional fear and what is an actual survival fear. The emotional ones are the ones that hold you back from living your true, purposeful life. Always be aware of your thoughts and make decisions based on whether you are living from your values and whether they will lead you to your ultimate life that you know is true to your core.

Surround yourself with an empowering environment (people, places, media, thoughts) to give you the best opportunity to live your life, that is the right one for you. Only you can decide what that looks like. Go forth with love in your heart.

Grace Vassallo is a Salon Business Coach from Melbourne, Australia

Inspiration 301

Desire

My desires are sacred.

I desire ...

Inspiration 302

Space Between Thoughts

Vanita Dahia

I am a crystal, pure, uncontaminated and vibrant. I can heal and colour the world as I take up the colours around me. As I take on the colours, I am capable of taking on many identities and express joy, sorrow, pain, or happiness. Turbulence of incessant thoughts and worry places my mind into a kind of habitual "jungle mentality," which I might identify as stress. Shall I warehouse the negative thoughts or re-habilitate them? Let's rip the stress band-aid off and nurture the mind.

When you're next finding yourself in the pitch-black closet clutching your dark thoughts, remember you're not alone. Others are peering through the illusion of control keyholes looking for a brave soul to bust the closet and truly live.

In a lyrical and funny way, be authentic, take the armour off, get out of your comfort zone and be yourself! Pause to deepen attention in the space between thoughts and connect with the very presence and compassion that can inform intelligent action. Consciously become aware of the space between your thoughts, dwell in them and elongate each space with blissful peace.

Vanita Dahia is an Integrative Medicine Pharmacist from Melbourne, Australia

'Go To India Where it All Began.'

Margaret Hepworth

It was a voice that spoke to me in the liminal moments between sleeping and waking: 'Go to India where it all began.' Just like that and clear as a bold whisper. I sat up in bed, not questioning the voice, instead the purpose. Where what all began? Buddha? Gandhi? Hinduism? What?

I had already stepped out of my safe and secure world of teaching; already asking life changing questions: 'We need more people experimenting with peace and non-violence. What would happen if we equipped our young people with the tools and strategies for peace building?' But where was this 'voice' taking me now?

Within six months, I found myself in India. Within two years I was running workshops in peace-building across Melbourne, India, Pakistan and Indonesia. The Gandhi Experiment had begun!

I believe we should all learn the art of connecting with our inner voice. We each have a big idea locked away inside us. We simply need the key to unlock what is holding us back. That key is found through connecting with our inner voice.

So listen. Listen carefully. Then go to your 'India', where it will all begin for you.

Margaret Hepworth is an Educator and Author from Melbourne, Australia

Touched by Recovery

Luciane Sperling

'Recovery is the healing process of your subconscious bringing wisdom to your conscious, helping you to restore your heart, reminding you to truly and honestly become the best version of you and achieving your full potential in life.'
– Luciane Sperling

WE CAN NOT solve problems by using the same thinking pattern you were using when the problem was created, or you will create yet more problems. Recovery is not going to be easy, because facing yourself requires big courage. But I'm telling you, it's going to be worth it. Remind yourself that hardships often prepare ordinary people for an extraordinary destiny. The recovery process will guide you to love yourself again, discover that you can trust yourself and take care of your happiness regardless the situation around you. You can find out that what you really need is to nurture your body and your spirit.

Owning your story and loving yourself through the process is the bravest thing that you will ever do, because life will always offer you another chance.

At any given moment, you have the power to say, 'This is not how my story is going to end.' I am investing in myself to be able to serve people around me and live my life with purpose, and be a valuable figure to the community.

Luciane Sperling is an Author, Inspirational Speaker and Global Entrepreneur from Sydney, Australia

Life is a Piece of Cake!

Heather Belle Murphy

Dear One, Life can be a Piece of Cake but first you must choose the cake you actually want! Then assemble the ingredients, follow the recipe and hey presto! You get that Cake! What if you decide you don't actually want that Cake? Choose another one and make that! What if you don't know what to choose? How about reading up on inspirational women and for the time being model yourself on them? Many Women don't get around to choosing a Cake and wonder why they end up with a Mud Pie! A job/life/relationship they hate! And because that is familiar, many people confuse complaining and "feeling bad" with taking action toward creating a better future.

It's not all our fault by any means, common challenges include: poor role modelling, societal disempowerment, financial disadvantage, trauma affecting our emotional threshold and hormonal programming generally. Women can become overwhelmed by the curve balls which Life throws at us resulting in limited choices and poor habituation; or addictions which are commonly used to "manage" anxiety. Worry is like being on a rocking horse: it gives us something to do, but doesn't get us very far!

My Life began to change dramatically for the better when I actioned my first Love-Life Plan.

Heather Belle Murphy is a Life Love Money Mindset Coach from Melbourne, Australia

Inspiration 306

HOPE Will Never Fail You!

Jane Logue

Hope can be easily defined as an optimistic attitude of our mind based in our expectations of all the beautiful positive outcomes related to any circumstance in our world. This world that surrounds us with so much different events and feelings related to those events.

Life was taken from me in 2015, my independence, my job, my real me as woman and as a mother. I had Sepsis and almost died: I was in the space between life and death and I thought I would not get out of this! Sepsis took memories away and causes pain and chronic fatigue syndrome. I miss myself so much!

Faith in God and hope has shown me the other side of it: the learning to bounce back, to be resilient, to find strength, to keep walking! Sometimes thoughts of suicide pop in my mind, but I know I need to be strong to fulfil my mission and the time this life has given to me. Hope is holding me: one day I will be free again! And I will shine on the other side of this path much wiser!

My hope is that one day humans may spiritually progress to live better without feeling sick first, living with love and peace, protecting people and animals against any cruelty. We are all creatures of God and with hope and faith, any cure is possible! Life has now a new meaning for me.

Regardless of the problem – Fight with Faith and Hope, because you have those skills in your soul – we are the winners already!

Jane Logue is a business owner from Sydney Australia

Inspiration 307

The Sacred Goddess Promise

Maria Jesus Romero (MariPosa)

I promise to honour the Divine Feminine Goddess within. I promise to chart my own course, willing to meet whatever comes because I have trust and faith in my journey. I promise to enable the wellbeing and the empowerment of others, but I will also refuse to subject myself to negative energies and have boundaries set to protect myself and my valuable energy.

I promise to listen to my own inner knowing, and that sometimes this will mean breaking the rules made by others in order to be authentic to myself. My truth comes directly through my heart, and I will use my mind as the servant to manifest it. I promise to remember that life is an ever-changing flow from one moment to the next and I willingly go with that flow, and be like a river. I promise I'm deeply connected to the earth and I stay close to nature, I recognise that I am not separate from it. Being connected to nature is essential for my health and wellbeing. I promise to always raise the sisterhood up, and celebrate the beauty and power within other women, as I will celebrate the beauty and power within myself.

This is my promise…

Maria Jesus Romero (MariPosa) is a "Sacred" Goddess Healer, Green Witch, Medicine Woman, Red Tent Facilitator from Melbourne, Australia

Inspiration 308

I Focus On

NATURE

The Greatest Gift

Kerry Upham

The greatest love of all, the love of self is not always easy to achieve. Words from the song *Greatest gift of all* (Written by Linda Creed, Michael Masser) have a powerful message. I suggest you search them out and listen to them. In fact put it on in the car and sing out loud to the song. It's very uplifting!

We live in a world full of words and images that rob us of self-approval and self-love constantly. Take every opportunity to praise and approve of yourself.

Find your strength from your internal center where you feel and know the safety and security that is you; that is LOVE.

Kerry Upham is a Completions Practitioner; Coach; Counselor; Speaker; and Co-Author from Melbourne, Australia

Beautifully Broken

Ramona M. Pinckney

There was a time when my mind was blurred, and I wore weariness like a garment. I was once a child whose days were once filled with laughter and joy, but life was never the same after being touched by evil. Those days were gone. Shame became a constant unwanted companion. Lost and wandering in a desert of loneliness, I walked a path of teenage pregnancy, suicide attempts, and chronic depression. I was imprisoned by the pain of my past and fear of the future. Mistrust destroyed relationships, and each new relationship was viewed as holding potential for harm.

I had gotten lost. All that remained were the ashes of a broken spirit. When I was at my lowest, someone pointed me to Christ. I am so glad that I put my trust in Him. Jesus became the one person in my life that never forsook me. He knew my faults and loved me anyway. Yes, I was broken, but I was beautifully broken. Through my shattered life, God's light shined and the darkness was chased away. Jesus took the shattered pieces of my life and made me whole again. Jesus gave me a "crown of beauty instead of ashes," and He will do the same for you.

Ramona M. Pinckney is an Author, Speaker and Nurse Practitioner from South Carolina, United States

Inspiration 311

Beauty

I am learning to see the beauty within myself.

When I look in a mirror I see ...

Inspiration 312

Home

Monika Miller

Your wisdom within
Ignites your inner knowing
Where kindness and strength of heart
Leads you on the path that you are going
When overwhelment and frustrations grow
Breathe, go general, stop, guide your thoughts
Mindfully climb up the emotional scale, show your heart what it already knows
You were born amazing. You are not broken. You are searching and sifting
Your discomfort is your barometer, your inner compass
Thoughts are the engine and emotions are its fuel
The law of life – no need to keep score – yet you keep record as it passes
Each experience good or not is a chance for renewal
As you learn, grow and expand you will see
Trust your inner wisdom, the one that says, "You can do it" its nature's gift to you
Life is truly meant to be enjoyed, to achieve all that you can and want to be
You, the creator of your world, can dream big and have it too
Believe in your special gifts as they are only yours to have
You are universal loving energy that is gifted to each of us
You are an important piece of the big puzzle that guides us all home

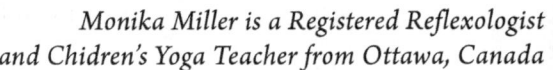

Monika Miller is a Registered Reflexologist
and Chidren's Yoga Teacher from Ottawa, Canada

Inspiration 313

Liberation

Helen Beeby

The notion that the status or happiness of a woman depends on her partnership with a man has vexed women since the 19th century. Probably longer. In my 20s I remember feeling irritated by a male colleague (after I said I was feeling a little down) when he hinted it would all be better when I essentially 'found a man.' It is hard to be a liberated woman with such comments. 'A woman needs a man like a fish needs a bicycle,' is as indignant as it is witty.

How can one interpret the experience of womanhood and personhood simultaneously? Bridge the gender gap, break the glass ceiling, yet maintain female strengths and nurturing qualities? Eternal questions.

Maternal empowerment is a buzzword in world health discussions at present. Good, as I've never felt more alive than when I was giving birth. For me, it was where the physical met the spiritual with a primeval force. The fulfilment of a biological purpose with no equivalent for men. Both sexes can go into space, fight wars, cure diseases; but only women can have babies. It is a major privilege, inspiring and empowering.

Harriette Hartigan said it best: *"Giving birth and being born brings us into the essence of creation, where the human spirit is courageous and bold and the body, a miracle of wisdom."*

Perhaps it's easy to be a woman.

Helen Beeby was a Journalist for 18 years in the UK from Mornington, Melbourne

Inspiration 314

Let Go and Grow

Maxine Palmer-Hunter

How long do you plan to hold on to past pain?
How long do you plan to hide behind the hurt?
How long will you bear the grudges that consume you ?
How long will you live in wrath?
Yes You Queen !
One of the hardest lessons to learn is letting go.
Whether it's guilt, anger, love, loss or betrayal .Change is never easy.
We fight to hold on and we fight to let go.
You feel that your challenges right now are greater than others. No one understands your pain .Your frustration. Your sadness. Your anger. It's okay to feel this way BUT for how long. Let Go and Grow
You are special and your presence is unique
Don't allow the obstacles of life to emerge you into an overwhelming burden of emotions .Life has a time limit and you only have one shot at it .Make it COUNT
Things will not be forgotten but the negative emotions that stop you from growing and living your best life can. Find a lesson in that experience. Find a strength that has emerged Let Go and Grow
Cry, Wallow, Scream, Shout,
Then GET UP and Bask in your UNIQUENESS and SHINE
Let Go and Grow.

Maxine Palmer-Hunter is a Educator, Director, Author, Speaker and Mentor from Birmingham, England

We All Have Special Needs

Carlyn Ryklief

A childhood marred led to my interest in what makes humans do the seemingly inhuman. In 1963 Stanley Milgram at Yale examined justifications for acts of genocide offered by those accused at the World War II, Nuremberg War Criminal trials. Perpetrators all find excuses, from the schoolyard bullies to psychopaths. Though personally motivated by emotional special needs, the term extends to the physical and cognitive. Teachers largely address the latter two. I have worked with students whose diagnoses included Down syndrome, Autism, Hearing loss, Developmental Delay, Undines Curse and Rhett Syndrome. But perhaps most special needs are not diagnosed. Relief from acute shyness, despair, fear, depression, anger, emotional pain are only addressed during extreme displays. Developments in neuroscience and social neurobiology increasingly reveal genetic, physiological, chemical and childhood experiences influencing thought and behaviour.

I've learnt:

- What is most personal, is most universal
- Every act of communication is an act of translation.
- The genetic difference between humans and chimps is less than 5%,
- The genetic difference between the most and least gifted person is 0.1%
- I've never taught a child with special needs, who hasn't taught me more.
- We all have special needs.

Carlyn Ryklief is a Teacher from Gisborne, New Zealand

Flower by the Road

Marlene Richardt

In 2005 I made a big choice: to leave my marriage of 16 years. For me this was the biggest decision in my life. I thought dying would be worse than leaving my marriage; I wasn't thinking clearly or rationally and the war in my head was raging out of control. Yet somewhere deep inside, I knew that if I stayed a part of me would be lost forever. And so I left.

Fast forward ten years and I'm happily married to my soul mate. I live on 15 acres in the countryside, am five minutes from the beach, I do yoga every Friday, and hike through the gorgeous countryside every second Wednesday. I have a beautiful fur baby called Bella, I work six months of the year and spend the rest of the year surrounded by nature.

Now my message is this: when you come across a decision that you think is too hard or hurts too much – but you know is right for you – acknowledge the fear and do it anyway! Once you have uprooted yourself from a situation that doesn't fulfil your deepest yearnings, you can be transplanted somewhere the impossible becomes real. You can be a flower by the road.

Marlene Richardt is Executive of her own life, from Hikurangi, New Zealand

Inspiration 317

Find Peace

Robyn Harrison

Find Peace: Allow some time to be still and quiet. In my experience life has always been busy, often with not enough time to stop and recharge.

I've always prided myself on working well under stress, and seemed to function at my best with pressing deadlines and endless to-do lists. However, I discovered through my life some of the most wonderful things have come about as a result of giving myself a time-out. After a shock diagnosis of both my parents with cancer, followed by providing care through their final years, I gave myself a big time-out, alone. Within a week of my mum passing, I was heading to the mountains – an environment where I could focus purely on myself. For one week, with no plans or expectations, what was going to happen was purely about me. Since then, finding my quiet place has taken on a greater importance, and my time-out now can happen anywhere and anytime I need to recharge.

Remember, you have everything you need within you to accomplish what you want to do, but you will gain so much more throughout your life and for all those who share your life, if you travel peacefully and allow yourself the time to listen to your own rhythm. Just breathe and find some peace.

Robyn Harrison is an Artist and Teacher from Sydney, Australia

Inspiration 318

Wake up!

Rachel Gaia

I am Woman. I am YOU. I fought so hard to be equal. I am educated, proud. I climbed the corporate ladder, in a male dominated world. I won!

Technology is my new efficient limb. I am ruled by time. Rush, Rush! 'Hurry, we'll be late!' 'Oh, first I'll answer that text.'

Tic Toc Biological clock. Beautiful, squishy Baby … TORN … is it impossible to survive without a dual parent income? Did I create a world without choice? Get back on the wheel … I love my career …

Daycare, School, University, 9-5. The Cat is in the Cradle watching YouTube on his smart phone.

The Digital Generation cemented its foundation. Why experience life, when I can observe it on my big 52-inch Panasonic? Breathe …

The earthy scent before the first rain touches the soil, skipping through the forest, chorus of cicadas, exploring caves, digging for worms, dirt under my nails, catching tadpoles in icecream buckets, scraping knees, sliding into the creek, children's laughter, hanging upside down from the lowest branch … adventure without limits. Are you awake now? Do you remember? … They do … Earth's Song is in all of us.

Take off your shoes child … hold my hand. We step out the front door. I am WOMAN. I am YOU. I AM the EARTH.

Rachel Gaia is an Entrepreneur and Music of the Plants Specialist from Melbourne, Australia

Inspiration 319

Good Impressions

Aylee Sunstrom

You don't get a second chance to make a good first impression. Our eyes tell our brain multiple stories within seconds. Judging and assessing is the innate intelligence within human beings designed to keep us safe.

The story others form instantaneously about you, can make the difference between acquiring the position/promotion, achieving the sale; engaging the audience; being taken seriously, securing the relationship. etc.

Take time regularly to evaluate your appearance and your presence, then assess whether they are in alignment with your true essence, your highest values and your deepest desires.

Let your "outer" reflect your "inner": amazing things can and will happen.

Aylee Sunstrom is an Image Consultant from Melbourne, Australia

True Mirror

Ana Bogdanovska

With our eyes we can see everything except ourselves, for that, we need a mirror. As long as we look in the wrong mirrors, we will only have destruction.

It takes a lot of courage to look in the mirror and accept what we see. There is no mirror in the world that shows us what we want to see, we just have to look in the mirror and accept what we see ... because what we see, whether we like it or not, is what we are.

Ana Bogdanovska is a Master of Laws LL.M. from Skopje, Republic of Macedonia

Inspiration 321

You Matter

Glyn Conlon

Do you think that good looks are a benefit? In my 20's I crippled myself with comparison and perfection. My radar picked up those who criticised; proof I was not perfect. Don't spend your precious time proving who's right and who's wrong. I see now I hesitated unless I thought I was perfect. Staying small benefits no one.

Have the courage to disagree respectfully and interrupt gracefully; you won't need to listen to one more word than you want to. Know your boundaries and change them if they no longer serve you. When I learned how to listen to my own thoughts with compassion, my stories no longer held the power to create health issues and my world became productive.

Spend time practicing the art of self-empathy; self-soothe if there's no-one around. Listen to others and practice compassionate assertiveness without being intimidated or defensive.

Calming the head talk and walking towards vulnerability give you the glue that holds your body-mind health together. Load your life with others that value and enjoy your company and who are willing to communicate that clearly and often

Glyn Conlon is a Compassionate Communication Specialist from Sydney, Australia

Gratitude Dinners

Rosemary Teed

Gratitude dinners happened once per week (at a minimum) when our three children were growing up. It was a special time because we all sat down as a family to eat together, to just be a family.

When we first introduced the idea of gratitude dinners, our children were a little perplexed, as they could not see the difference between saying thank you and being grateful. Initially, we asked them to think of just three things like being grateful for the dinner, the clothes they were wearing and the fun time walking the dog that day.

Then, it was such a joy because they all wanted to be the first to share and it was no longer limited to just three. They realised themselves there were so many things to be grateful for in their lives.

Hanging in our home office is a gratitude poster from our children when they were all under 13 years. It reads: "We are so grateful for the fantastic time we had together! We all loved the water skiing. We enjoyed spending time with you guys. We love you heaps."

Our gratitude dinners still happen today, with as much enthusiasm as when they were children.

Rosemary Teed is an Entrepreneur, Speaker, The Courage Creator, Author/Family Therapist from Melbourne, Australia

Inspiration 323

Inspiration

From reading this book of Inspiration I am more inspired to ...

Inspiration 324

Tenacity

Lisa Sweeney

I was born lucky – but I never let that sap my enthusiasm. Some lucky people want to survive on luck. Not me. Luck runs out. I want to thrive on tenacity.

Tenacity is not letting go when everyone tells you it's not possible. Tenacity is staring the naysayers in the eye and gently letting them know you can. Tenacity is being prepared to make mistakes and take the right advice and learn and make a few more mistakes and learn some more and take some more of the right advice. Tenacity is putting a smile on your face when your world is going to hell in a handbasket. It's standing tall with your shoulders back ready to face the next obstacle, the next negative, the next pain in the neck you wish you'd never met. Tenacity is overcoming adversity, overcoming rejection, overcoming the bad days we all have. Tenacity is being prepared to do your homework so you're inspired to take a calculated risk. It's seeing something scary and daring to take it on because you've done the planning that enables the self-belief to have a go.

Above all, tenacity is a good night's sleep because regret keeps you awake.

Lisa Sweeney is a Strategic Connector
from Melbourne, Australia

Success is Personal

Tracey Maclay

"Take chances, make mistakes, that's how you grow. Pain nourishes your courage. You have to fail to learn how to be brave."
– Mary Tyler Moore

Scottish mother in-law, aged 80, when asked what to pass on: "Get your priorities straight. Education is important. Work to pay for it if you have to. Being poor, we were sent out to work to bring money into the family. Staying on at school was not an option. Choose your company wisely. You don't have to follow the crowd. If you're feeling lonely, still don't follow others into bad habits just to fit in." I really wish I'd had that advice at 21!

Listen more, talk less. Talk to the elderly and learn from their past. Listen to who you truly are. Let go of fear and be responsible for your own actions. An art teacher wrote on my assignment once, "It would make me turn in my grave if I knew you were serving cups of tea instead of using your fine mind." I remember this still. I was a single mother at 22. I overcame domestic violence, anxiety and depression. I worked and finished two degrees, had two children, divorced, lived alone until I remarried in 2015. I have eventually made a meaningful life for myself and found my soul mate. Strive to be the best version of yourself that you can be, then love will find you.

Tracey Maclay is an Early Childhood Teacher and Yoga Teacher, from Brisbane, Queensland

Inspiration 326

Admire and Inspire

Kristie Dean

I believe everything in life happens for a reason just as you have picked up this book and opened this page. Life will give you signs and lessons, which you must be quiet enough to see and hear. So, I say good luck bad luck who knows? Observe your life, more than getting stuck in it. Flow with life and live more in the moment, as they say the past has gone and the future hasn't happened, I know it's easier said than done, but that's what I think we are truly here to master. There is a different energy in my life, when I accept what is and understand it's not the universe trying to fight me and make things difficult but guiding me, through the important journeys my soul is here to experience.

When you feel, your heart beating inside you and you're quiet and still enough, you will feel the answers come to you, guiding you to your next journeys. Admire and Inspire other women, never come from jealousy, we are here to grow and love each other, your female relationships will be the most powerful ones you will ever have, so always respect and honour them as that reflects who you truly are. So today buy two red roses, one for you and one to be given to a woman you admire. As we are all truly amazing so shine bright and let life show your destiny. Always Admire and Inspire! Leaving a little of your Sparkle as a foot print, where ever you step.

Kristie Dean is a Massage Therapist and Author from Perth, Australia

Embrace New Chapters

Janet McNeill

I am woman – by Helen Reddy – lifts me when I am down.

My marriage broke up and I plunged into despair – my future had suddenly gone, leaving me empty with no direction. During the separation, the loss of my mum to cancer – after battling for five years, nursing her to the end, followed then by the loss of my home, then my father, my horses, dogs, and cats all were taken in by my brother who lived four hours away. I had to cope with leaving my large home on acreage, to move to the city and survive in a tiny two bedroom unit all alone.

The three years I spent here were both the best and worst years of my life! Worst because of what I had lost! The best because of what I had gained. I found freedom to act spontaneously, have time to help others, exercised furiously, volunteered to help others, forced myself to go out and meet people and made some amazing new friendships.

Sometimes in the midst of sorrow, new opportunities present themselves. Life does not end just because a chapter closes – a new one begins, embrace change and discover your passion.

Janet McNeill is a Real Estate Agent, Director, Author and Volunteer from Mornington, Australia

The Chameleon

Maxine Palmer-Hunter

Bullying was rife towards me, especially in the last year at primary school and the first year of secondary school, every day I lived in fear. They lived on my estate ... I would be trembling on a daily basis – yes, I was teacher's pet, and they loved my endearing nature, but was that my fault? I was a young child with an old soul who had experienced so much already, whilst displaying a masked confidence. I quickly had to find my own strength if I WAS TO SURVIVE MY LIFE.

I joined the athletics club, netball team, rounders team and swimming club. I learnt to play the recorder and the guitar and I started Aikido classes. I was a class prefect and teachers always found me helpful.

It's so important to be liked ... Right? By the time I was 13 years old, I could take no more ... Death was the only way out. "Set me free. Take me from the wilderness. No more pain."

Well it did not work ... here I am, reliving the tale. I found the paracetamol, went to my room and took some – oh yes, tonight all my troubles will be over. I laid down on the bed, waiting to be whisked to heaven, no fear. Let them see that I was worthy, but no longer felt so. Well, five hours later, my eyes pinged open. As the years have gone by, I realise that the extra layers on me have been a protective shell. If I covered myself enough ... Don't give up

*An extract from chapter in *Pain to Purpose* Anthology.

Maxine Palmer-Hunter is an Educator, Director, Author, Speaker and Mentor from Birmingham, England

Inspiration 329

Have Courage

Jacinda McIntosh

Living in Hong Kong for five years I found myself at times feeling lonely, isolated, trapped and depressed. Arriving in Hong Kong I didn't know what to expect. I was apprehensive and worried about how I would cope with the language and culture differences. We lived in a village in a small apartment with two young children. We were surrounded by swampland and wild buffaloes. The village had no car access which meant we walked every where, which was a struggle in the humidity. A far cry from where we had come from.

Many days I felt trapped and yearned for home. I would spend a good part of my day pounding the pavement, that would alleviate the negative thoughts and keep me going.

I am very grateful to have had the experience of living abroad, even though it was the most challenging time of my life. I learnt a lot about myself, and made some wonderful friendships.

During our life time we are all faced with adversity and unexpected challenges, but I learnt no matter what life throws at you we all have inner strength, it's just knowing how and having the courage to tap into it.

Jacinda McIntosh is a Personal Stylist
from Melbourne, Australia

Inspiration 330

Be the Lighthouse

Melissa Groom

Everything we have been through in our life is a gift. Whether it was joy, hardship, adversity, tragedy it has made you the amazing, beautiful, soul you are today.

We have a responsibility to share our stories and share our gifts of wisdom with the world. It is up to us to share our learnings with the world and shine the light so bright so that others can find their way out of the darkness.

Light the way, set others free, to release the pain so that they can be the best they can be. Let them soar, and spread their wings, set fire to the past so a new life can begin. You were born to be the lighthouse, to heal others, to open their eyes to see the beauty in life and in themselves. Your words are so powerful. They can heal, they can give hope, they can change lives, even save lives. Show them the path, guide the way to peace, love and happiness. Show them how magnificent they are. Help them remember the perfect, amazing, beautiful soul they are.

Creatrix changed my life and taught me to be the lighthouse. Thank you Maz Schirmer – The Institute of Women.

Melissa Groom is a Business Mentor from Kingscliff, NSW, Australia

Inspiration 331

Transformation from Childhood

Katerina Egglezos

"You may encounter many defeats, but you must not be defeated. In fact, it may be necessary to encounter the defeats, so you can know who you are, what you can rise from, how you can still come out of it."
– Maya Angelou

The transformation from a young girl to an empowering women is monumental. When you are a young girl, you have dreams and compete with each other. When we are women, we have a vision and empower one another. I have had the privilege to have such strong and inspiring women in my life who motivate and influence me to become the person I am today.

My Godmother has had a tremendous impact on my life. She has supported me and taught me valuable life lessons. She has taught me to always try my best, no matter the outcome, as your best is all that matters. Her bubbly personality and humour enlighten me, and her positivity through everyday encourages me to be more like her. She shows great resilience and has taught me how to always bounce back after getting knocked over.

"Vitality shows in not only the ability to persist but the ability to start over."
– F. Scott Fitzgerald

Katerina Egglezos is a Student from Melbourne, Australia

Inspiration 332

Listen to Your Heart

Jo Schutt

I grew up in a town where everyone knows each other and sport is the activity of choice. At age 13 I met a 16 year old introverted and highly depressed musician, which resulted in me disconnecting from the world.

At 18 health problems led me to a Naturopath and I discovered I had an innate understanding of the body and nature. At 20 enrolled to get my Bachelor of Health Science – Naturopathy. We moved from country to city and I was constantly out of my comfort zone, but thriving. I loved meeting new people but my then boyfriend's lifestyle choices began to have a destructive effect on his health and relationships and we gradually grew apart. At 22 I met someone who introduced me to fun, love and connection on a level I had not experienced before. He showed me what was possible and I felt like I was living for the first time. I made the heartbreaking decision to leave the person I'd been with for over half my life. I had to let go of feeling responsible for another person's health and happiness and start focusing on me and my future.

I met amazing new friends I began to reconnect with family and self again. At age 40 I have not been single since 13 and I have wondered if I'd missed a crucial time of personal development being on my own. But I discovered that the right person will allow you the space to be you, to spread your wings and grow as an individual.

Jo Schutt is a Business Mentor and Growth Facilitator from Melbourne, Australia

Inspiration 333

Intention

I intend to ...

Inspiration 334

Embracing Change

Joanne Whalen

"Be the change you want to see in the world."
– Gandhi

We often say we are ready for a change in our lives. But are you ready to be that change you want to see? Positive changes come by taking consistent conscious action. It means being aware of your thoughts and feelings and changing them into what you want to see and become.

It means taking your excuses and turning them into your reasons. It means hard work and dedication. Writing down the changes you want to see and become and creating a plan. Implementing your plan step by step. Rinse and Repeat.

When you are aware of the changes you want to see and become, the outcome is spectacular. Visions become clearer, attitudes become more positive and uplifting, energies become more alive and vibrant.

So live your dreams and embrace all the wondrous changes you are about to endure. After all you only have one life to live.

Joanne Whalen is an Entrepreneur and Professional Network Marketer

Inspiration 335

No Regrets

Christy Amalu

What advice has a significant woman in your life given you, that has stayed with you over the years, to impact your life in a positive way?

My mum taught me never to look back in regret but to move on. A setback is never a bad experience but another lesson learnt.

Then one of my aunties taught me that no matter the challenges life throws at me, I should not look a sorry sight.

Christy Amalu is a Clinical Nurse Advisor from Milton Keynes, United Kingdom

Inspiration 336

Allow Grief

Debbie Singh

Even though you are still standing, you really don't know how. Although you emerge through the thick fog of isolation and pain, the dark, empty, lonely place which stifles your breath and even though you may function in day-to-day tasks, you are incomplete, broken and changed completely. Life has knocked you down before, but nothing like this, this pain is so raw, such deep sadness and heartache wondering "how long must I weep". Is this what they would want, for you and for me? Or can we move on and live life once again, knowing all they would want is for us to be happy. This Love is so deep that it lasts forever and although it changes us, it moulds us and shapes us, as our lives become barely recognisable, yet still it remains.

Allow grief to mould you into the person you are meant to be. A beautiful new version of you and me, there is so much of life for you yet to see, carrying your memories locked up within, you are free to move forwards, not because your pain never existed, but because you were never meant to remain in that place called Grief.

Debbie Singh is the UK's No.1 Grief Coach from Wolverhampton, UK

Inspiration 337

Ten Things

Natasa Denman

Others tell me they get tired of just observing what I do. They ask how I do what I do with three children under seven and a 7-figure business. I travel for business, pleasure and run around doing what most mums do. I require tons of energy. Here are the 10 things that make all this happen. Apply what resonates with you and see your energy skyrocket:

1. Find out what your core need is and fulfil that daily. For me it's significance so by inspiring other daily this gets me going.
2. Have no option but to get results – I am the only bread winner in our family so that pushes me to perform daily.
3. Exercise minimum four times a week.
4. Eat light and small – sugar and complex carbs will drag you down, avoid them 80% of the time.
5. Take regular holidays.
6. Reward yourself regularly – no point in working hard without rewards.
7. Find out your top strength through Gallup Strength Assessment – this is where your gold is hidden.
8. Focus on one day at a time and sometimes an hour at a time to avoid overwhelm.
9. Get eight hours of sleep.
10. Find a support network and ask for help regularly.

Work Hard – Play Hard. That's how I do 100 events per year!

Natasa Denman is the Ultimate 48 Hour Author from Melbourne, Australia

Inspiration 338

Change Comparison Into Inspiration

Miranda Powell

Comparing ourselves is a natural part of being human. I, myself, am not immune to it. After some searching, I realized: The power of a single story is immeasurable.

So where do these thoughts arise? From my experience, it is from lack of self-love. I am aware of this since I went through a terrible experience in my life, where I felt like I didn't measure up in my achievements as much as my friends, family etc. I started to compare my weight, looks, the list goes on! We are usually comparing the worst things we think about ourselves to what we think is the best part of someone else.

So how do we not compare?

- Be aware when you are comparing. No one is perfect.
- Focus on your own positive aspect!
- Commit to growing and advancing yourself.
- Focus on your own path.
- Be Grateful! Gratitude helps us to change our energy.

Comparing ourselves hurts us, especially emotionally. It is important you stop this habit. See your own individual light and what you have to offer. Embrace your individuality.

Miranda Powell is an Angelic Intuitive and Empowerment Coach from Virginia, United Statess

Syrian Refugees

Cille Harris

"We are Citizens of the World."
– Epictetus 55-135 AD

On a recent vacation, I blogged about our trip while weaving in the teachings of the Greek philosopher, Epictetus, from the book, *Art of Living: The Classical Manual on Virtue, Happiness and Effectiveness.*

When I returned home, my friends asked me which lesson I liked the best. "Citizens of the World" was very powerful for me and I still marvel at its relevance today. There are so many heart wrenching stories of refugees in our world, especially from Syria. We wanted to do something meaningful to help a desperate situation. But, what could we do in our tiny village? We contacted the nearest centre that was sponsoring refugees and offered our support. We enrolled as volunteers, donated money, went to meetings, followed their progress and delighted when the first Syrian family arrived.

That summer we invited the family for a visit to our community, in rural cottage country. Our families enjoyed a picnic lunch, a walk through the woods and an afternoon on our dock, boating, swimming and sharing life experiences. No boundaries, no borders, just people enjoying each other's company. Citizens of the World

Cille Harris is a Facilitator from Ompah, Canada

Inspiration 340

Today and Tomorrow

Monika Miller

What is one piece of advice you would give to your younger self?

If I was to go back in time and give my younger self advice, I would say, life is supposed to be good. You are a work in progress, be easy with yourself. You are meant to be here. The world needs you! Your hardships are only there to help you realign to who you are.

You are valued and loved.

Monika Miller is a Registered Reflexologist and Chidren's Yoga Teacher from Ottawa, Canada

Choose to be Strong

Carla Fogazzi

As a business owner since 2003 I help businesses understand bookkeeping. I find that bookkeeping is the black sheep of the business family but I'm hoping to change that. I was married at 21 and came to Australia as a 36 year old Italian without any English, and had a 10-year-old daughter. My marriage was great at the beginning, then became physically and mentally violent; moving to Australia was a sea change – the physical behaviour stopped but mentally it continued.

Over five years I learned English and started with a secretarial course, then worked day shift in a factory and spent three nights a week at Chisholm until I completed a Certificate of financial services. I started my business in 2003 part time while I worked for others part time, building it to four staff by 2006.

After my divorce, I helped support my daughter until recently, pouring money into her home and wellbeing and I was happy that she and her husband invited me to live with them in 2015. After a year, I found myself homeless, after a terrible argument about money.

I now have a dual Diploma in Marketing and Business Management completed 2016. I'm 57 and I'm a survivor, no matter what happens in my life. What I want to say to other women everywhere is that no matter what happens, you can make the choice to be strong, to be happy and look at the positives in life.

Carla Fogazzi is a Bookkeeper from Melbourne, Australia

Sheer Persistence

Faye Waterman

"I can do things you cannot, you can do things I cannot: together we can do great things."
– Mother Theresa

Courage, persistence and determination have taken me places in life that have given me the strength to take that walk on the wild side and be on purpose and love what I am doing and doing what I love.

Having a voice and supporting women to tell their stories through simple conversation allowing a shift in paradigms and become the greatest them. Over the last 6 to 7 years one of my achievements in life has been working with women who have lived with family violence. My book *Hidden Truth Why Suffer In Silence* is the voice of women telling their stories. These women are now living the lives they deserve.

On many occasions, with my life at risk helping to create a voice for these women, who have lived with violence, helping them realise there is real help available for them. Allowing them to live a life that is now filled with purpose. As a woman with imperfections I am now significantly comfortable and in the right place to create the changes that will give a voice to women in the future.

Helping women find their passion to shine.

Faye Waterman is a Radio Producer and Author from Melbourne, Australia

Inspiration 343

Reflect

Reflecting back on my year, allows me to feel ...

Inspiration 344

Second Chance

Melissa Griffiths

Sometimes life gives you a second chance, take that chance. Life is very short and even though most of us know this we fail to recognise this. We fail to realise how precious life is.

My life defining moment was when I made the decision to be true to myself and live as a transgender woman. It was my second chance in life. I took that chance and began the process of transitioning from male to female. As a result, I made new friends and lost old friends. By believing in me I found my inner strength and grew as a person.

I have had new experiences on my journey, some great, some not. People either laughed at me, poked fun at me or have admired and inspired me. Whilst sometimes I laughed it off at other times I cried buckets of tears alone.

Still I never gave up or stopped believing in me or the journey I had embarked upon. I knew I had to be courageous to keep going and draw upon my inner strength. The ability to draw upon our inner strength is something we all have. So when life gives you a second chance, take that chance to a beautiful new life.

Melissa Griffiths is an Auditor
from Melbourne, Australia

Inspiration 345

The Undiscovered

Virginia Phillips

"Broken Crayons are unique and create beautiful masterpieces."

The undiscovered works of art surround us every day. Inside a brand new box of crayons is a world full of possibilities. Black, brown, brilliant rose and white are just a few. All of them engage an imagination allowing dreams to come alive. The mere loss of just one element can diminish the opportunities for a masterpiece to earn praise or positively impact the others.

If just one crayon rolls off the table, drops to the floor and lands in the shadows of darkness, marred and broken; a hand, must reach down, past a normal comfort zone, to find this crayon. Then grab it, dust it off and lift it up, if it has any chance at finding glory. It is okay if it doesn't look like the others because originality can hatch new vigor, smiles, laughter, and love. Unveiling, a precious heart and soul.

These true colours create the possibility for passion to exist and are the fuel needed to create something beautiful for the next box of crayons.

The world needs to discover what is inside your box of crayons. So, open them.

Virginia Phillips is an Author, Speaker and Personal Coach from Colorado Springs, USA

Inspiration 346

Listen to Feedback

Christina Sanchez

Take criticism seriously, but not personally. If there is truth or merit in the criticism, try to learn from it. Otherwise, let it roll right off you."
– Hillary Clinton

When I was growing up, and well into adulthood, I would take criticism, constructive or not, very personally. I would become defensive, I would not listen but rather retort right back with a criticism of my own. I would then hold a grudge or even cut that person out of my life completely, saying to myself that they were jealous or mean. In some cases, I would even talk about how mean they were and how they had "done me wrong", trying to form a posse of people who agreed with me and reinforced how mean and nasty the other person was. But one day, as I was rounding up a new posse, one of my very good friends said, "Christina I love you and I want you to be happy. He is right. Now for once stop and think about what he said and sleep on it."

That was the first time that I began to look at criticism as a tool for growth. That has helped my personal life and business life immensely; now when someone gives me criticism, the first thing I do is view it as feedback then I think of this: If one person offers criticism I ask around, because maybe they are jealous, or being mean (yes there are people like that). If two people say it then I stop and take a look at what was said and if it applies. If I hear it from a third person I consider making some changes.

Christina Sanchez is a Womens Business Coach from Canberra, Australia

Embrace Pathways

Hazel Theocharous

In life there will always be at least two pathways for you to follow, knowing which one to choose can be daunting. But always remember you do have a choice. My life so far has taken a number of different pathways and on each one I have encountered difficulties and rewards, much like most of the wonderful women I know. The one constant for me is for me to be me.

When I moved from one country to another with my family, it was one of the most important pathway choices I think I have ever had to make. But despite all of the differing thoughts going through my mind, I made it.

Apprehension at the packing stage, then excitement at the thought of seeing Big Ben and Buckingham Palace for the first time changed to feeling of sadness and homesickness when thoughts of home kept arising. I realized that the moving on of my life, friends and business had to take second place to my children, helping them through the uneasy transition to a new place, a new world to them. Three years on, everyone has settled and happy and I have a new pathway leading to a new business choice and a dream ready for me to fulfill my passions. Sometimes you need to follow a new pathway to reach a choice or a dream you hadn't realized yet.

Hazel Theocharous is a Small Business Coach and Trainer from London, United Kingdom

Inspiration 348

The Power of Persistence

Andrea Donaldson

"Persistence helps us to reach our destination and through the process of that persistence our character is built."
– Travelling Home: A Flight Plan For the Journey to Joy.

In the year 2000 my husband and I were blessed to adopt a four year old boy and his six year old sister from Ethiopia. While visiting their birth country to bring them to Australia, we discovered they had an older sister. She had been omitted from the adoption in error. We knew straight away we were meant to adopt her too. The obstacles put in our way were many and the process took six long years. There were times when we almost gave up, but now nearly ten years after she arrived I am so thankful we persisted.

Persistence and the support of others were the key to complete our family. Do you have a dream in your heart that cannot be shaken? Expect to be tested as you move towards it. And keep going. For us, a little girl on the other side of the world was depending on us to never quit. We had to keep asking questions and seeking answers. Be sure that if this dream is God-given, He will also give you its completion if you are prepared to do your part and persist.

Andrea Donaldson is an Occupational Therapist from Melbourne, Australia

Inspiration 349

You Are Your Own Destiny

Neenah Olivier-Stewart

The universe takes us down many pathways, one may be blocked but another will be open. So take a step back and follow another path.

You can only get stronger by taking many paths, so don't give up, and keep moving forward; but remembering that sometimes moving back is in order to find another way. Learn as you walk through your journey of life.

We can all make this world better by staying positive, helping others in their journeys by inspiring, nourishing, protecting, healing and guiding in the right direction.

- Stay positive, work hard and make it happen!
- Dreams and goals can be met by you!
- You are your own destiny!
- Trust yourself, your intuition is real!

Neenah Olivier-Stewart is a Beauty Therapist and Mum from Mornington Peninsula, Australia

Inspiration 350

Your Suffering is Your Gift!

Lillian Benrubi

A difficult statement to swallow, I know, but let me tell you a story. Forty two years ago, the sexual abuse stopped. It was a relief that someone "seemed" to care enough to notice, (how it felt to an eight year old), to stop it, and make a difference in her life. At this young and tender age, children don't often have the power, or the voice, let alone the understanding to put an end to what seems like an incomprehensible experience. But a therapist and coach was born, as a result of the work done to heal, following this event.

A compassion for others, that no man or woman live a life unseen or unheard, became the stand for which that 13 year old girl stood, the age of a near death experience and when she decided she would become a therapist. Making a difference in her life and those of thousands of others, is the purpose that gives meaning to her life. Breaking through barriers ... using her voice that was once inaudible, to speak a truth that heals, is empowering to all.

Suffering is not without purpose, it is your gift!!

Lillian Benrubi is a Psychotherapist and Coach from Newmarket, Ontario, Canada

Inspiration 351

The Power Of The Dream

Piera-Angela Bottari

I believe in the POWER of the DREAM ... a desire so strong, that you will find a way to achieve it, it may take months or even years, but nothing should put you off, although many will try to crush your dream and you are never too young to dream by saying, don't you need money, education, looks, skills etc. Think outside of how people think ... you will probably find ways that others haven't thought about ... so you will tell them other ways of getting what you want..there are people who will continue to say no, and you will find one person who will say, yes, why not ... and that's how the POWER OF THE DREAM WORKS. Keep moving towards it, little by little, and keep that vision in front of you ... be confident and you will have it, dont give up ... the world changes, rules change. What you can't have today you may have later.

I was a poor Italian migrant child ... I was always a dreamer. I achieved all my dreams without money, skills or support. You Can Do It Too!

Be my inspiration and never give up. Write and tell me of your achievement.

Piera-Angela Bottari is a Motivational Speaker for Youth and Therapist from Brighton, Melbourne, Australia

Inspiration 352

My breakthroughs have been ...

Inspiration 353

Small Daily Activities

Linda Clucas

What has inspired me. I was given a book called *The Slight Edge* by Jeff Olson one Christmas. It took me a few months before I even picked it up. And when I did start reading it, I couldn't get into it. Do you ever find that happens to you? Some months later I thought I would try to read it again. This time, I just devoured the book. Even now, some years later, I find myself picking up the book from time to time and re-reading parts of the book.

Why? *The Slight Edge* is a way of thinking that enables you to make the daily choices that will lead you to the success and happiness you desire. It's about doing those small things every single day, consistently every day that will lead to success.

It's about doing those small things that you don't want to do, but you know you should do every day. Since reading *The Slight Edge* I have developed a passion for personal development, either by reading or by listening to audio books and podcasts. I have made a commitment to myself to do 15 minutes of reading or listening, six days a week. Whilst that doesn't sound like much, in today's fast-paced world many of us don't have a spare 15 minutes. However, I know that 15 minutes feeds my brain. I have developed a passion for learning. It's easy to do, and it's also easy not to do. You make the choice every day.

*Linda Clucas is a Professional Network Marketer
from Melbourne, Australia*

Inspiration 354

Family Life and Obstacles

Merlene Crossfield

I grew up in a little town called Cavaliers. We were one happy family, Mom and Dad's relationship was from school days, home was blooming. Mom and Dad were in love, my grandmother invited her to the UK from shilling days and she did not go because she wanted to be with him. Later, my mom found out that Dad was having a secret relationship with Mom's friend.

My little brother died suddenly, Mom was now in a state of shock, I felt sorry for her. Dad left not long after my brother passed away, to live with Mom's friend. Home was not the same again, my mom was now left to face the tragic situations on her own, I could not offer any assistance. Mom and myself, were always in heated arguments, our relationship was rough, once in a while we would have a smile.

Mom or Dad didn't tell me that they loved me, until I became an adult. I had parents but I was lonely. She would hit me with anything she could find, machete, leather belt, sometimes uncalled for, she told me curse words too. I felt I had no purpose in life. I cried and cried. I hated her but I had to I succumb to all. I thought my mom had hated me, it took me years to find out that she was suffering inside. I prayed about the obstacles and forgave her. If only I had known how beautiful my mom was on the inside and outside. Now we are best friends, I love her I give honour to her the most wonderful woman in the world.

*Merlene Crossfield is a Support Worker
from Birmingham, United Kingdom*

Inspiration 355

Perfect Peaches

Lisa Linton

A ripe, juicy, just picked peach – what could be more perfect? Dita Von Teese said, "You can be the ripest, juiciest peach in the world, but there is still going to be someone who hates peaches."

Women can become obsessed with what others think of them. We can be focused on presenting ourselves as someone who is well liked, successful and popular. The fact is that no matter how thoughtful, kind, and generous you are, there will be people who just don't like you. To make matters worse, often with no good reason at all.

When we strive to achieve our goals and are worried about what others think it is a distraction and a barrier to our success. In many cases these thoughts sabotage us before we even take the first step. In reality the reliability of our interpretations of what others think can be vastly different to the facts.

So instead of concentrating on moulding yourself into the illusive perfect peach, why not focus on being the best you can be and not be worried by what others think. When challenges come your way, focus on your dreams rather than letting thoughts of what others think take you backwards.

Lisa Linton is in Leadership Training from Melbourne, Australia

Inspiration 356

I Focus On

GRATITUDE

Take Your Own Path

Joelle Wörtche

I knew very early that I wanted to study economics, in order to take over, someday, my mom's company, where I worked and helped since I was little. So it was very obvious that I studied economics after I finished school. But throughout the illness of my grandmother two years ago it was up to me to take care of her. Because of her dementia it became very fast a fulltime job and I had to stop studying. During that time I was able to take some classes in marketing and communication and found my new passion for writing.

One year later I was able to study again and started with journalism and I am more then happy with my decision. The journalism brings a lot of variety within and I learn many things that will prepare me for future tasks but furthermore it became my passion.

Plans are changing without asking, this experience is one, that mostly all of us have to face someday. Plans are made to be changed. Some paths are leading and some not, but each step leaves a footprint behind and if you look back someday, these footprints show your own path and where you came from.

Joelle Wörtche is an Online Journalism Student and Co-Owner from Babenhausen, Germany

Inspiration 358

I am...

Eleni Ikon

Two of the most powerful words, for what you put after them shape your reality. Life becomes less complicated as we learn to reveal our true selves. In all of life's interactions learn to express the true you externally, by remembering internally I am…

Honest, With integrity, Authentic, Confident, Interesting, Generous, Positive, Strong, Fearless, Loving, Devoted, Faithful, Compassionate, Sympathetic, Beautiful, Forgiving, A leader, An achiever, Intelligent, Unstoppable, Professional, Amazing, Unique, Powerful, Independent, I am Courageous in my convictions.

I AM WOMAN!

Others opinion of me does not define who I am. When we stop trying to be the person we think others want us to be, we will find more time to simply love and accept ourselves for the person we truly are.

Decide today what you will become and how you will live. That which we do not confront in ourselves we will meet as fate.

LOVE and LIGHT

Eleni Ikon is an Entreprenuer, Life Motivator from Melbourne, Australia

Inspiration 359

Dream

Christine Stow

There must be a dream! If you want to get to somewhere different, you need to take a different path. If you want to get there, you first must have a dream. You need to be able to dream it to do it.

After finding my daughter had a rare muscle condition, my life took a different turn, it was not the life I had dreamed of. All along I believed there must be a way to dream a different dream – to step up and step into your Power – to dream a dream and make it happen.

Even though my daughter is totally dependent on me, I took my life on a different journey. I stood in State and Local Elections, wrote my book. I could stop to smell the roses.

So even though, my life has taken a different turn, I can still have dreams and make a different pathway.

I CHOOSE that pathway. I choose to find joy in my life and fulfil my dream of helping others step into their power.

Always have a dream.

Christine Stow is a Speaker, Author, Carer Strategist from Melbourne, Australia

Inspiration 360

Reflections

Michal Stewart

Look
How far
You have come
As you reflect
On your life's progress
Small beginnings gather
Momentum till here you are
Discovering who you've become
And what made you who you are today
Realising now how much you have grown

Experiences learnt along the way
Steer your future in the direction
And at the pace of your choosing
Little steps become long strides
Confidence grows stronger
Believe completely
By staying true
To yourself
You have
Peace

This poem is written in the Etheree stlye of poetry which was devised by American poet Etheree Taylor-Armstrong (1913-1994)

Michal Stewart is a Healer from Melbourne, Australia

Inspiration 361

A Real Woman

Gina Collins

A real woman is whatever the hell she wants to be! At 18 and the oldest of four children, I decided to move from the country away from family and into the city as I knew I needed more opportunities. Little did I know that not long after they would move so far away that it was impossible for me to see them for nearly 10 years, I would have to go it alone.

I married early, had three beautiful children whom I adore and was home with them for 10 years, performing as a singer at night for some extra dollars, studying different courses along the way.

Once the youngest started kinder, it was time to get into business. I re-evaluated what I needed in life and made a concerted effort to not have anyone in my life who didn't make me feel good. Simple. After 19 years of marriage, the last to go was my husband. A wonderful man that just wasn't fulfilling what I needed.

The past eight years have been, in short, amazing. I have visited many countries for both work and pleasure, sang on huge stages, founded and sold three businesses and have a wonderful new partner. I was bird in a cage, but now am living the dream, anyone can do it.

Gina Collins is an Eco-friendly Educator – Health, Beauty, Environment, from Melbourne, Australia

The Infinite Joy of Being YOU

Shivany Gonell

"Follow your bliss and the universe will open doors for you where there were only walls."
– Joseph Campbell

Do you have the courage to run with the dream that picked you? Or will you let it get away and slip through? We have been given a gift that we call life, so don't blow it. You are not defined by your past; instead you are born anew in each moment. If you don't run with your gift, not only will you sell yourself short, but you also rob the world of you.

What is right for one soul may not be right for another. Look deep within your heart. Don't compare yourself. The more you are willing to follow your inner guidance, the happier your life will be. You are here to follow your Soul's calling.

When you say yes to your Self, yes to unconditional love, yes to freedom, yes to wisdom, yes to truth, yes to abundance, yes to light, the planet will become a more loving and peaceful place. If you want to see the change you need to be the change first.

Shivany Gonell is a Psychotherapist, Healer, Coach and Psychic from Cairns, Australia

Inspiration 363

"Hey, You! Yeah, You!"

Laura Abrams

Hey you, yes you! You are the beautiful woman with a smile that helps to bring brightness to the world, right? If you are shaking your head, "no," then you surely fooled me. Want to know who I see when I look at you?

I see a woman with a heart of gold, a captivating personality and a beautiful mind. I see a daughter who is making her parents proud. I see a woman who works hard at whatever is put before her. I see a woman with a nurturing nature, gentle healing hands, and a kind spirit.

I see a woman who hates her entire appearance and envies others. I see a women who feels over looked and under appreciated. You are treasured by so many. I see a woman who looks in the mirror and sees her own worst enemy. She sees flaws when that's what makes her unique.

Hey you, yes you! Come borrow my unbiased mirror and see the truths. Come see the woman whose value cannot begin to be measured.

Hey you! Oh, you know it's you now? I'm glad that you finally see the woman whose smile helps brighten the world. Go and set it aglow.

Laura Abrams is an Entrepreneur from Spring Hill, United States

Inspiration 364

The Unexpected Experience

Zynoe Bahat Abrahams

As a young parent I suffered from depression and just couldn't seem to deal with how fast my life had changed I had so many things I wanted to do, goals I wanted to accomplish before having to take care of someone else other than myself.

I had to firstly accept that things often don't work out the way you want rather the way it's meant to be. Secondly I told myself that I need to turn every obstacle in my life into something positive. And always believe that it's never too late. I told myself that no matter how things turn out differently I should not be held back or let down.

I started thinking that if I should want to do anything for myself right now it would be selfish. That my time had run out because I had my son and that it's all about him but I realise that if I'm not happy how could I raise a child to be happy? If I gave up what advice can I give him growing up?

So today I live my life with something my mother once told me, "I'm the only one who can create the change I want to see, it's all up to me." In life, women sometimes have to deal with difficult situations and we often find it hard to deal with our emotions but we were created so strong and beautiful that we can always overcome hardships.

Zynoe Bahat Abrahams is a Homemaker from Cape Town, South Africa

Inspiration 365

My Story, My Journey

Patricia Earle

"Not all of us can do great things, but we can all do small things with great love."   - Mother Teresa

From the narrow confines of Belgium to England, to multi-cultural, multi-everything Birmingham. Joining the WFWP and becoming involved in the concerns of women, peace and interfaith.

So shy in the beginning, meeting with 2 or 3 women, and now having 100+ women in my home. God giving me the strength and passion to bring women together from all races, cultures, religions/no religion, social backgrounds, ages. One big family, one heart beating, putting our differences aside, feeling our common humanity and aspirations for peace and human dignity. Listening to each others' stories, feeling the heart of oppressed and abused women, families and communities broken by violence and conflict. Young people yearning and longing. Creating a safe space for women to share their heart, their joys and sorrows. Learning to listen, be humble, to realise that God works through people of all religions. So much in common - birth, cycles of life and death, happiness and sadness. Going beyond our faith into that sacred place where God is.Empowering and praying for each other, for our world. Learning to forgive, to let go. Doing things together, travelling to the Holy Land, building an orphanage in India, helping the needy, in hospital, refugees. Making friends, getting rid of fear and prejudice, showing compassion.

Patricia Earle is an advocate of the WFWP - Women's Federation for World Peace. She lives in Birmingham, United Kingdom

Thus we are all connected. Congratulations on reaching the end of *The Book of Inspiration for Women by Women*!

It is often the invisible, the unseen threads of love and support that are the strongest and most powerful. Although you have reached the end of *The Book of Inspiration*, it is by no means the end. The doors to endless possibilities await you to create your life with love, confidence, conviction, faith and powerful support. Go back through the pages of *The Book of Inspiration for Women by Women*, find or rediscover those passages that pulled at your heart strings and start doing something with them. Take that step forward, leave inaction behind. Each woman and girl in this book has your back, cheering you on.

We invite you to connect with us. Share and reach out for more if you feel the need. Share your wins and your challenges. Above all, go forth and be inspired and inspire. You have a gift you must share with others. Start reading the *The Book of Inspiration* again and allow us to be a part of your journey – it would be a humbling honour.

Use the following pages to reflect and create a plan of action for you and your life.

Thank you for stepping into our journeys, for allowing us to share and make a difference in the world. We welcome you to connect with us via the pages and at www.ruthstuettgen.com

With Love and Inspiration from all the Contributors in

The Book of Inspiration for Women by Women

About the Creator

Ruth Cyster-Stuettgen decided to create this compilation after recognising the value of inspiration in her own life. This book provides an arena in which women share their collective wisdom, their stories and their insights into life.

Ruth writes: "I've been a single mother, juggling work and personal life, recovering from a long-standing abusive relationship of 23 years.

This experience of self-discovery led me to author *From Misery to Mastery: Journey to Freedom and Empowerment,* a 'how to' book to get your life back on track after experiencing adversity.

I realise that I wasn't in control when I decided to leave. I felt an inner knowing in the pit on my stomach that I could not stay another night in the house with my husband. I needed to move immediately while he was out, taking my children and myself. All of my reasons for staying dissolved; where my children were in school, whether the timing was right, avoiding stress for them. On that one day I changed the world I knew and I left, never to return.

This huge decision was the catalyst for a new life, where yoga, meditation and steps that I've detailed in my book became core to who I am. Being given this moment of divine guidance, I now feel supported no matter what I'm going through. I believe strongly in the Law of Attraction in that it guides us to a place of being our best higher self and in total alignment with our divine purpose.

There were struggles but in amongst it all friends, family and the universe supported me and I know now that my role in this world is to serve others in the same way.

What I wished for most of all in that time was someone who could hold my hand and support me, showing me that everything was in flow. I wanted someone who had my back while I changed so dramatically, always encouraging me forward with grace. I found that help through coaches and mentors and I learned how to offer the same.

As I was helped, supported, coached and inspired, I found that many women could offer their own insights to help others grow and create their own joy. And so this book was born. May it give you joy and inspiration.

Ruth Stuettgen
www.ruthstuettgen.com

Reflection & Looking Forward

Real & Raw Conversations with women

Would you like to be featured as a Guest on inspiredwomanTV where you get to
- Share your message with the world?
- Inspire and encourage other women?
- Grow your reach internationally?

Professionally branded videos will market your brand message and be distributed on inspiredwomanTV channel and other platforms.

Join inspiredwomanTV channel at http://bit.ly/IWTV_YouTube

Express your interest at: http://bit.ly/IWTVInterest

From Misery to Mastery – Journey to Freedom and Empowerment

by Ruth Cyster-Stuettgen

- Change your life situation around anytime using powerful strategies.
- Discover the WOW-Factor hidden deep within you to step up and shine.
- Embrace your experiences, be empowered to use them to master your life.
- Ditch adversity and create your life on your terms not someone else's.

Special Reader Offer:
Claim your complimentary E-Book Version at support@ruthstuettgen.com (value $9.99)
https:/www.ruthstuettgen.com

I AM NOW
A True and Personal Story

A Western Australian Girls Personal Memoir, touching topics with raw life survival stories designed to touch the hearts of many. Shattered by sexual and mental abuse, surviving several major car accidents, Cancer at 29, the fight for her life was on. International mum, New York to deep in the Amazon Jungle / experiencing plant medicine, IVF journeys, losing 30 kilos, healing suppressed childhood abuse…and turning pain into power! Follow her journeys in this powerful, inspiring book.

"I AM NOW"
Order now at
www.kristie-dean.com

- Do you love travelling?
- Can you imagine exploring new cultures and countries?
- Do you dream of travelling and experiencing Life?

Discover the world's best kept travel secret, The ultimate and exclusive VIP Lifestyle Travel Club. Go to
http://bit.ly/inspired2travel
click on Nr 2 and find out how

YOU too can be inspired to travel more for less.

Imagine freedom, feeling the tension in your body releasing, a calmness blanket slowly and easily spreading over your shoulders, neck and chest.

Peaceful joy quietly perculating deep down in your heart. How can you tap into to this feeling more every day?
Sign up for my free online mindfulness seminar today.
Contact Kinder Living, Monika Miller at

www.kinderliving.ca

Hand Drawn Artwork

Light and Love xx
www.aligreerart.com

Calling all Trade Companies
Are you Sick Of Wasting Your Time and Money?
Only competing on price and losing tenders?
You know There Has to be a better way
WWW.WINWINTENDERING.COM
INFO@WINWINTENDERING.COM

Vision, Mission & Values Our Vision

Soroptimist International is a vibrant, dynamic organisation for today's professional and business women. We are committed to a world where women and girls together achieve their individual and collective potential, realise aspirations and have an equal voice in creating strong, peaceful communities worldwide.

Our Mission is to inspire action and create opportunities to transform the lives of women and girls through a global network of members and international partnerships.

Our Values: Human rights for all - Global peace and international good will - Advancing women's potential - Integrity and democratic decision making - Volunteering, diversity and friendship.

Soroptimist International South West Pacific invite you to become a member to help us serve women and girls across the globe. www.siswp.org

---

The Magical Getaway Foundation is the only national charity dedicated to giving first ever holidays to vulnerable or disadvantaged Australian children and their families to improve their health, physical and emotional wellbeing to reach their full potential.

We work with children and their families affected by domestic violence, along with other issues such as mental health, abuse and poverty.

1 in 3 Aussie kids have never been on a holiday, not even a weekend away.

Please contact Rosemary Teed, Founder/Director, for further information.

www.magicalgetawayfoundation.org

www.reclaiminnerpeace.com   www.chrisoulasirigou.com

www.triumphhrc.com.au

www.thecarmgroup.com.au

Thanks for supporting this global project of *The Book of Inspiration for Women by Women.*

www.ingramcontent.com/pod-product-compliance
Lightning Source LLC
Chambersburg PA
CBHW081226080526
44587CB00022B/3844